1/01/2015

1y 17/2016

WHAT OTHERS ARE SAYING

"I am the sibling of more than one autistic person. I too am 'on the spectrum.' It is rare to find someone who can so eloquently express what it *is* to be autistic. I cannot pretend to know the struggle of Matt and of his mother, for my autism is 'high-functioning.' This book, however, made me *feel* as if I could understand and know what it means to love, or, be, or teach a 'moderate/severe, mostly non-verbal' autistic person.

Since the dark time in the 1970s when my mother, fighting for her struggling youngest son, was told: 'There's nothing wrong with him. He's acting this way to get attention. He's too smart for his own good,' to 2013 when we *all* know someone with autism, the way is increasingly being lit and guidance and support is available. It is people like Liz Becker who are lighting the path. *Every* teacher, every parent, and every coach should read this book. It would be a good idea for everyone else, too."

—Kay Schwink, PhD, Teacher

"Thank you, Liz, for sharing Matt's world with the rest of us caught up in the journey of autism! This book shares all the raw emotions of both laughter and tears that go along with the autism world. I've followed Liz's blogs for a while now and this book is the ultimate compilation to years of challenges in parenting an autistic child. I'm definitely recommending this book to anyone who is raising any child with special needs!"

—Esther Flores, Parent

"I met Liz, Matt and Christopher about twenty-six years ago, before Matt was diagnosed with autism. I remember when we dropped a pan on my front porch to see if Matt could hear. At that time, we both hoped Matt's lack of communication was due to a hearing loss. I hope those who read *Autism and the World According to Matt*, recognize the hours, days and months Liz spent in the early years invading Matt's world through play therapy and talk, talk, talk…

I am an Exceptional Student Education Specialist for a public school system. This family's compelling journey will be a recommended read to my colleagues as an example of what a child with a moderate-severe autism disorder is truly capable of achieving, both in a supported home environment and in the general education setting. Trying to figure out how to assist a child with this type of communication disorder to reveal what they really know (especially with communication being the focus of a Common Core Curriculum) is the bane of the classroom teacher. Just as Liz and her family demonstrated time and again through reflection and adaptation, teachers of students with autism will also need to reflect and adapt tasks to unlock the full potential of these unique students."

—Margie Powers, MS,
Exceptional Student Education Specialist

"Author Liz Becker has done a tremendous job of pulling some of the most significant moments on Matt's journey from childhood to adulthood as an individual with autism. As a consultant and a district coordinator for autism, I have been asked by so many parents and teachers, 'Is there a light at the end of the tunnel? Is there hope for my child/student?' Liz's response would be a resounding, '*Yes!*' She speaks of Matt's abilities rather than his disabilities. So many times, parents and educators focus on the can'ts rather than the cans. Liz tells an amazing story of her son Matt, who she did not force to be anything but himself. She wasn't focused on normalizing him, but helped him to work through his own uniqueness to cope with everyday life. Her down-to-earth true stories will at times make you laugh, bring tears to your eyes, and most of all let you see that yes, there is hope. Thank you Liz for sharing Matt's story with parents and teachers who desperately need hope for the lives they lead and the work they do!"

—Michael Hinsley, MS Ed.,
Consultant and District Coordinator for Autism

"Just an example: 'It's not easy pulling thoughts from Matt's mind. It's a complex interaction that must be carefully choreographed.' She gets the fear of failure, the pain of imperfection, and the courage. If we'd put ourselves in the minds and skins of our children for one day, to feel what they feel…we just might see what heroes they are. So much hope…

I clung to Thinking in Pictures when my son was diagnosed with PDD seventeen years ago. It gave me *hope*. Son-rise by Barry Kauffman made me realize it was hard work. This generation of mothers of autistic children has a new book to guide them. It's real…and there are so many things Liz gets about autism."

—Rosemary B. Walker, Parent

"Autism can be like a country without a map. Liz Becker has trekked through the world of autism with Matt. Her collection of essays is enlightening and encouraging. Special education teachers and health professionals, especially, need to avail themselves of this resource that Liz and Matt have made available to all of us."

—Sue Keller, Parent

"I have had the great pleasure of knowing the author and her two boys for many years. I have seen her fight for Matt using strength, grace, and courage to insure his continued growth. This well-written book is inspirational and educational for all parents! Her honesty with a perfect pitch of humor is a great read as we all struggle to understand and encourage children to find their happiness how ever that may look in their world."

—Marilyn Rockovich Garnto,
School Pychologist, Librarian

"A must-read for teachers, parents, siblings or anyone who is interested in autism. Becker balances the insight and curiosity of a scientist with the love and compassion that only a mother knows. She navigates and expands the boundaries of autism with humor and sometimes a few tears. *Autism and the World According to Matt* takes the reader on an inside journey of a family that beat the odds by working together, insisting on equality, and knowing when to push and when to relax. By the end of the book, you will be rooting for Matt and will walk away with a rare insight into a fascinating and beautiful world."

—Bryan Michael, Teacher

AUTISM AND THE WORLD ACCORDING TO MATT

AUTISM AND THE WORLD ACCORDING TO MATT

A collection of 50 inspirational short stories on raising a moderate/severe, mostly non-verbal autistic child from diagnosis to independence

LIZ BECKER

TATE PUBLISHING
AND ENTERPRISES, LLC

Published by Tate Publishing & Enterprises, LLC
127 E. Trade Center Terrace | Mustang, Oklahoma 73064 USA
1.888.361.9473 | www.tatepublishing.com

Tate Publishing is committed to excellence in the publishing industry. The company reflects the philosophy established by the founders, based on Psalm 68:11,
"The Lord gave the word and great was the company of those who published it."

Book design copyright © 2014 by Tate Publishing, LLC. All rights reserved.
Cover design by Jim Villaflores
Interior design by Jimmy Sevilleno

Published in the United States of America

ISBN: 978-1-63367-455-4
Psychology / Psychopathology / Autism Spectrum Disorders
14.10.10

To the grandmothers

Shirley Howard
Your curiosity was so very welcomed. Autism awareness starts at home.

Marion Johnson
For showing acceptance and love. You were always willing to make his world a little brighter.

Thelma Edmonds
For practicing the acceptance of his differences that most others could only preach. For truly seeing that my son was different, not less.

ACKNOWLEDGMENTS

As THE SAYING goes, it takes a village to raise a child, and my own little village of family, friends, teachers, and support staff all helped Matt to become the wonderful young man he is today.

I wish to thank my husband, Tom, for being my rock when I needed one, for being Matt's father when he asked you so sweetly and tentatively if you would be his dad. I want to thank my oldest son, Christopher, for stepping into the role of mentor and hero for his little brother and for being the fierce force to be reckoned with if anyone sought to harm him in word or deed. I want to thank both his stepsiblings, Jacob and Sarah, for taking him into your hearts and accepting him into their extended family as if it were as natural as breathing.

I want to thank my friends—Becky, Margie, Kay, and especially my dearest friend, Carol. All of you were always there when I needed you, whether I needed to vent, hear words of encouragement, or just needed a hug.

I want to thank all his teachers for their willingness to think outside the box and be creative in both their methods of teaching and in evaluation, and Matt's paraprofessionals, his aides, Jane and Pat. Both were heaven sent, showing patience, love, and a willingness to learn about the mysterious condition of autism in order that they could enhance his ability to learn. I also want to thank his speech therapist, Debbie, who worked with him for over seventeen years. Matt is able to speak as well as he does because of this wonderfully patient woman.

I especially want to thank my son, Matt, for revealing to me the beauty and simplicity of life. You have taught me more than any other experience of my life, and I will always be so very thankful to have the honor of being your mom. Lastly, and most importantly, I wish to thank God for giving me such a beautiful child, for showing me my son's indomitable spirit and courage, and for trusting in me to be the sole light in navigating the unknowns of autism.

CONTENTS

FOREWORD

As a mother of an autistic child, it was a happy coincidence that I stumbled across Liz Becker on Twitter one rainy afternoon while searching for fellow writers of all things autism, and I am so very glad that I did. I am also incredibly honored and slightly shocked that Liz asked me to write this foreword, so I promise to do my best.

Simply put, the book is an absolute joy to read. *Autism and the World According to Matt* tells of all the ups and downs during the life of a young man with moderate to severe autism, as told by his mother, Liz. The stories really resonated with me as a mother of a young child with an Autistic Spectrum Disorder, particularly the tales of when Matt was a little boy.

What I loved about this book was that it was uplifting while at the same time being full of practicalities and brutally honest. The overall theme of the book is that anything can be achieved and that as a parent, you know your child best, not the teacher or the health professional who may see your child several times a week. What Liz proves in the book is that if we give our children the tools and experiences in life from an early age, then they can reach their full potential.

What instantly struck me while reading the book was the incredible bond that there is between Matt and Liz. Most importantly though, she saw and still views the world today through Matt's eyes. You are sucked into their world from the moment you start to read of how life was for a young Matt. Liz openly tells of how professionals voiced their opinions that Matt would need to be institutionalized. She says in the book:

"In the doctor's next breath he recommended institutionalizing my son, adding he would be too tough for me to raise and didn't understand how difficult it would be on my family."

What you gain by reading the book is a wonderful insight into the world of autism, a world that spans over twenty-five years, but this is not a doom and gloom book, the realities are there and the nitty-gritty of living with a child on the autistic spectrum, but what shines through the book is Liz's optimism and her 'anything can be achieved in life' outlook, they simply pour from every page. It is very much a life story of how autistic individuals can achieve and contribute to society.

The special bond between Liz and Matt is shown throughout his journey. One particular story tells of how Liz took the plunge one day and allowed Matt to shop alone at the annual Labor Day flea market event in which fifty thousand people attended. Every parent of an autistic child will be able to identify in how this was such a huge step for both Liz and Matt. I read this story with a huge lump in my throat. Liz sums her feelings up beautifully:

"This would be the year that Matt was finally allowed to walk alone, shop alone, go where he wanted to go and just blend in...I knew in my gut that it was time and he was ready."

Everyone, and I mean everyone, should read this book, not just parents of children on the autistic spectrum. We all have much to gain and learn from reading about Matt and the wonderful journey that he has been on.

—Jo Worgan
Senior Writer
Autism Daily Newscast

INTRODUCTION
MY WORLD, ACCORDING TO MATT

MY WORLD AND my son's world are inextricably linked. When his life changed at the tender age of two and a half, my life changed right along with it. Matt has the regressive form of autism, progressing normally until around eighteen to twenty months old. A joyful and happy little boy became withdrawn and sad. He had begun to talk, saying the word "kitty" as he happily chased after our cat. Then in what seemed like just overnight, he lost his voice and his fascination with the cat. Arms began flapping, body spinning, lining up toys, averted gaze, no fear of danger, but fear of everything else. Communication between us was lost. We had to start communication from scratch.

Autism makes a child different than their peers in areas of learning, communication, speech, emotions, and even in health issues. It forces them to use very creative ways to learn to enmesh themselves into a world that can be confusing and sometimes hostile. The amazing thing is that they do and continue to move forward, against all odds.

Maybe Matt is different than other autistic individuals, but I doubt it. I know the autism spectrum is vast, with varying degrees of severity and symptoms, but I don't feel others can't learn and move forward as Matt has done. Am I being overly optimistic? I don't think so. I truly believe all children can learn. Sometimes it just takes longer and the road is more difficult, but learning remains dynamic—not static—regardless of his age. Each year I reflect on the accomplishments my son has made and set new goals for the year ahead. I find I am constantly in awe of my son; his perseverance and courage define him in my heart.

At diagnosis I was told that he was "moderately-severely" autistic. The doctor told me the only reason he didn't get the "severe" label was because he did not harm himself, other than that he was classically autistic, having every textbook symptom. They didn't wish to saddle him with the *severe* moniker, but they stressed his severity. In the doctor's next breath, he recommended institutionalizing my son, adding he would be too tough for me to raise and that I didn't understand how difficult it would be on my family. I bring this up to illustrate where we started on this journey. Don't assume that the reason he has done so well is due to a milder form of autism…don't assume any degree of autism is easy…and don't assume a child's autism will ever go away.

We have had our struggles and our bad days, but the good days outnumber them by far. You have heard the saying "It takes a village," and we met some great people along the way that had a wonderful influence on him—a village load of people. As a parent—to any child, not just an autistic one—it is normal operating procedure to try our best, learn about our child's needs, and seek out the right path. In comparing a neurotypical child to one who happens to be autistic, the only thing different in your quest are the specific needs and the amount of time devoted to those needs. For me, figuring out what he needed required me to understand what he was going through. It took lots of time, lots of observation, lots of trial and error, and above all else, lots of hope.

In 1988 these were Matt's symptoms as listed on his medical record.

SOCIAL INTERACTION

- Avoids eye contact
- Difficulty in understanding facial expressions or body gestures
- Lack of interest in people
- Lack of empathy
- Doesn't want to be held
- Anxiety in a crowd

COMMUNICATION

- Delay in, or lack of, speech, or echolalia
- Difficulty in starting a conversation or continuing a conversation
- Difficulty understanding sarcasm or humor in language use
- Appears not to hear, doesn't respond to their name

TYPES OF PLAY

- Spinning toys or just the wheels on toys
- Lining up toys in long lines
- Fascination with a particular topic
- A need for sameness and routines
- Lack of imaginative play
- Plays alone

SENSORY

- Reduced sensitivity to pain
- Hypersensitivity to sound, taste, and sometimes light

STEREOTYPICAL BEHAVIORS

- Body rocking
- Hand flapping
- Spinning

As Temple Grandin has said, autism is based on fear—fear of all the unknowns of this world, from how to communicate to reading facial expressions to trying something new. I understood his fear. I was gentle in my persistence to communicate with my son, and it paid off. Once he understood I was there to comfort him and fight the fears with him, the learning began. We moved ever forward, sometimes at a snail's pace, and other times with leaps and bounds.

Now let's look at my son as he is today—at twenty-eight years old:

SOCIAL INTERACTION

This is an area that we work on daily. He converses, even when it's difficult for him, and as he does so, he looks into your eyes. If you smile, he smiles. Matt has an interest in the people he knows and loves. If someone feels bad or is happy, so is Matt. I have found that Matt actually has more empathy than most neurotypical individuals. He cares deeply about his family, his pets, and his home. He will stand up to another person if he feels that person is wrong in their behavior, and he always champions for those whom he feels is weaker.

He is uncomfortable at times around people he hasn't officially met, but an introduction opens the door to acceptance. He can be in the middle of an enormous crowd of people he doesn't know without showing any signs of apprehension as he has learned to focus on other things. Actually, Matt enjoys the adventure of going out. Football games, flea markets, beachcombing…crowds are just not a concern anymore.

COMMUNICATION

In the early years, I was most worried about his ability to speak, as I knew the brain would stop attempting speech around five years old. If he didn't speak by age five, his chances of ever being able to speak would be minimal. I have read that 25 percent of all autistic children have no speech—that's a very scary statistic…and a very sad one. Matt began speaking just before his fifth birthday. We passed through the echolalia stage next (about two years' worth), and then his speech seemed to improve yearly. Although to this day he remains mostly nonverbal, it isn't because he can't speak. It's because it is difficult and confusing for him to do so. Over the years, he has developed a wonderful sense of humor, gained insights into neurotypical behaviors and speech patterns, and adapted his own behaviors to more closely resemble what he saw and heard. To this day his preferred communication is still in gesture, body language, and facial expression.

TYPES OF PLAY

As a young child, Matt spun toys and the wheels of toy trucks, trains, and cars. But as he learned new outlets for communication and imagination—in art, games, and books—the spinning stopped. Matt still has a fascination for particular topics, but he has expanded his interests to many new areas. Although he still likes to be alone for most of his day, he does enjoy being with others for short periods. Keeping to routines are mostly a thing of the past also (with the exception of Friday night pizza), and he relies on a daily planner to remove the fear of the unknown.

SENSORY

Matt still has hypersensitivity, and certain sensations can still cause discomfort on occasion. His showers are still lukewarm and his room dimly lit, but he doesn't avoid loud sounds anymore. He is still very particular about what he wears, especially on his feet, but he has overcome a tremendous amount of hypersensitivity in his clothing. He tries new foods—doesn't eat them, mind you—but he does taste-test. There's always that hope that any day now he could add a new food to his limited menu. Pain, unfortunately, is still an unknown. We are always vigilant for signs of pain because we are unsure if he would reveal his pain to us before it becomes life-threatening. There's hope that he will be able to reveal discomfort verbally someday. If told he has a cold, he will take care of himself with rest, fluids, and medication, all self-determined and administered.

STEREOTYPICAL BEHAVIORS

These are mostly a thing of the past. We haven't seen many of his previous behaviors in many, many years. He still paces when nervous or when something bothers him and stutters, trying to initiate speech.

Matt was the first autistic child to enter the school system in our area. No one knew what it was, and the misconceptions about what he was capable of abounded. Matt entered preschool and hated it. The teachers were not interested in his differences. He didn't interact, so they didn't either. He moved up to first grade for special education, and still the misconceptions prevented any real teaching. His lack of interaction was viewed more as disinterest than a social handicap. I began going to his class and talking with the teachers. Our biggest breakthrough came when the teachers watched Matt perform an alphabet dance—his body making each letter and in the correct order—that they finally believed Matt was a teachable child. Creativity in evaluation methods then led to acknowledgment of Matt's intellect. Learning became fun and exciting.

Matt progressed step by step, and as he did, the classic autistic behaviors disappeared one by one. He began speaking, writing, drawing, reading, and learning, and it seemed the sky was the limit. Matt graduated number four in his senior class, on the honor roll and a member of the National Honor Society. He won academic awards. His success paved the way for the many others that came after him. Teachers learned about autism from Matt and from me. Awareness was, and still is, everything.

I accept Matt for who he is, and I don't push him to change any particular behavior—instead I suggest various ways to achieve the things he wants and help him focus on the steps toward his goals. If he never changed another habit or behavior, he would still be the light of my life. It is Matt who chooses what to change, what to improve on, and what is fine just the way it is. When new challenges are met or old ones are overcome, we celebrate in this house—not because we want him to change, but because Matt sought to change. It's always a big deal, and it always has been. I recognize that he is continually trying to be the man he wants to be, and I am in awe of his courage and willingness to do what it takes to accomplish that goal. I can honestly say that his progress has been one unexpected joy after another, and that's because I remember where we started. Each year we fought battles, met challenges head on, and set new goals. It wasn't a picnic, but it wasn't all doom and gloom either. Life has been an adventure, and not just for Matt. I know I am a better human being for having the opportunity of sharing my life with this incredible young man.

Matt is currently twenty-eight years old and transitioning into an apartment of his very own, our ultimate goal since he was very little. What will the future bring? I know from watching him as he grew that that particular question can't be answered—but from looking back I realize that anything, *anything*, is still possible.

Many years ago I was asked if I believed in miracles. Without hesitation I replied, "I see them every single day." I was, of course, referring to Matt and the wonderful way each day provided some tiny step forward, some steps so small you would miss them if you weren't looking. I'm always looking, eager to witness that next miracle. Each time I see a small step forward, my heart is filled with hope that my son's dreams will be realized. For those new to raising the autistic child, I send you that same hope.

Hope that you see the tiny steps. Hope that you see and understand the courage it takes to make those steps. Hope that autism as a disability will not define your child, but autism as a uniqueness will be seen instead. Hope that your child's dreams will eventually be realized. Hope that you too will witness miracles every day.

HOPE IN THE SHAPE OF AN EGG

DO YOU REMEMBER Littlefoot and the gang from the animated movie series *The Land Before Time*? Littlefoot and his friends were baby dinosaurs separated from their parents, lost and trying to find their way to the utopia for dinosaurs, *The Great Valley*. This movie had two of Matt's favorite things: dinosaurs and babies. We absolutely had to buy the videotape for the original movie and for each sequel that came after.

Matt was still a wee one himself, between three and four years old. He would study his own features in a mirror, look at pictures of himself as a baby, and at some point made the connection that big people come from babies, and that there were small people that looked like him.

He made this connection by looking through a book I had on babies, one of those "your baby will be doing (some mile marker) at this age" book. It was filled with pictures of Gerber-type babies sitting, standing, and eating their peas. He would often ask for the book, using his pre-speech gesture, or a simple "baby" and a "gimme" gesture. A few times of me retrieving the text revealed its location, and shortly thereafter he would get the book himself. I always assumed he was comparing his face to those on the glossy paper, but now I think there was more to it than that.

As with all videos Matt loved, *The Land Before Time* was played over and over (and over and over) until everyone in the home knew each line by heart. One of his favorite scenes was Littlefoot being born, hatched from an egg. Ah! Eggs made babies. Matt watched his video and looked at the baby book almost daily.

One afternoon I found him on his bed with his hands closed gently around a treasure. "What do you have, Matt?" I asked. Slowly he opened his hands revealing his secret. There in the gentle cradle of his hands was an egg—yep, an egg. He looked at the egg and softly said, "Baby," as if the word itself could break his fragile treasure. The egg from our refrigerator, in his eyes, contained some baby dinosaur. He cupped the egg and slowly brought his hands together over the top, once again sheltering his egg. It was so cute!

Of course, now I had to decide whether to explain to him that a dinosaur was not really inside. Do I tell him that we actually broke open eggs on purpose and ate them—just like the scary, mean dinosaurs that chased Littlefoot and his friends? Nope. I wasn't ready for that. I certainly didn't want him thinking of me as one of the evil, bad guys, so I let him keep it for a while. I found the egg later that day, snuggled in a blanket. I picked it up and returned it to the refrigerator.

Each day Matt would retrieve an egg from the refrigerator and take it to his room to cuddle and warm. Each day I would find it and put it back until finally one day I realized I would just have to break it to him. I decided to show him. I took an egg from the refrigerator door and had him watch me as I broke it into a bowl. "See? No baby."

He was confused. There should have been a Littlefoot in there. Where was the dinosaur? I explained that this egg was not a dinosaur's egg, which would have been much bigger. I tried to explain that dinosaurs were extinct—gone from the earth—and there were no dinosaur eggs left to hatch. He seemed to sadly accept this demonstration and the crude explanation, at least for that particular egg. He sadly went to his room mumbling something about how I had *"gotten the wrong eggs."*

This is more than a simple story about a boy and his egg. There was more going on here besides Matt relating baby pictures to himself and to the characters in his movie. Sure, he had made the connection that every living being starts out as a baby, and that he was still a baby himself, but more importantly he demonstrated concern for his own "baby." He had saved the egg from the cold, cradled it lovingly, warmed it, and kept it safe. He showed empathy for a little lost egg.

This all came at a time when Matt seemed so oblivious to the rest of the world, didn't seem to want interaction, and appeared cocooned in an autism blanket. The simple act of taking an egg from the refrigerator showed that assumption was all wrong. Matt's display of empathy, caring for his unborn baby dinosaur, gave me what I needed most at that time, a glimmer of hope.

Hope…in the shape of an egg.

THE COVERT OBSERVATION

WHEN MATT WAS very young (and very autistic in his behaviors), he was an expert in the art of *covert observation*. Covert because he was subtle and oh so sly in the way he watched people's behavior and interactions. Matt didn't look directly at faces, as if to do so was just too painful. Instead, he averted his eyes to the ground or to the side. He would then take brief glances at faces or at the body language of another, just a flicker of his eyes, to take in all that he wanted to know. Do all autistic children do that? I know they all seem to look away or avoid faces, but do they all flick their eyes to covertly observe? Have you noticed this in your child?

I remember one sunny summer afternoon taking him to the park with his older brother, Christopher. Matt was only three or four years old. The park had all the playground goodies: swings, slides, sandboxes, tunnels, monkey bars, etc. Both boys ran toward the slides as soon as the car doors opened. Usually, I ran with them, but on that particular day, I decided I would hang back a bit and just watch. I was an "observer in training" back then, watching and deciphering Matt's body language, facial expressions, and vocal sounds (Matt was not speaking at that point). I felt I needed to become an expert at predicting his next move in order to avert any foreseeable trouble—and I was *extremely* curious. Why did Matt do the things he did?

I sat down on the bank surrounding the play area and started taking notes—I had come prepared with a laptop word processor my mother had given me. There were several children playing, their parents either helping them on the swings, or the monkey bars, or watching from a short distance while chatting with other parents. I watched the children too, but I took notes. What I saw was the usual dispersal pattern of playing children—usual, that is, except for Matt. He would always stand away from others, as if trying to keep a safe distance. At first it would seem as though he wanted this—wanted to be alone—but after a few minutes of watching, I came to the conclusion that he did not actually want to be alone; he was just unsure of how to proceed. He would stand at a distance with his head slightly downward, repeatedly flicking his eyes in the direction of his brother. He watched Christopher play and run and smile and interact.

Matt would then move slightly closer and repeat the covert observations on his brother. His hands would be twisting and turning as he stood there, a sign of high excitement. Matt would then get on the swings or go up the stairs of the slide where he would again flick his eyes toward his brother and the other children. Matt would slide or climb, but as he did so, he was also watching. It appeared to me that he was trying to covertly observe from as many angles of view as possible, as if he wanted to assure himself the behaviors and interactions he saw would be the same from each new viewpoint.

Was it a coincidence that during this same time frame Matt loved looking at himself in mirrors? He could stand in front of a mirror for hours, except he didn't just stand. He practiced facial expressions for sadness, and smiles, and angry eye expressions. He would kick a leg up behind him or raise his arms while looking in the mirror out of the corner of his eyes. Matt would try to see what he looked like walking, running, and playing. Was this because he had observed other children's body language and wanted to see if his own movements were similar? It was if he was asking himself, "Do I look like them?"

It finally dawned on me that Matt was teaching himself things I was not. I finally understood that although Matt could not speak, he could think—inquisitively. He was forming major questions, experimenting with body language, and trying to decipher human emotion and interaction—all of which require some major thought sequences. You could almost see his brain in the process of rewiring itself, trying to make up for the lost connections brought on by his autism.

I watched Matt, and Matt watched everyone else, but especially other children. He knew he was more similar to them than he was to me or any other adult. That right there, knowing he was a child, sheds light on his powerful thinking process. I knew from watching him as he maneuvered through these uncharted waters that everything I had ever read about autism (and at that time there wasn't much) was wrong. My son was not trapped in a world of his own, there was nothing wrong with his IQ, he was not lacking in empathy or emotion. My son was simply trying to open the door to learning communication and social skills—the same door that had slammed shut due to his autism.

Matt was standing right outside that door and knocking ever so lightly. It took some covert observations on my part to actually learn to hear his tapping, and finally learn how to open the door to his brand of communication. I realized that I was being watched. Every move I made, every expression on my face, everything—every single thing—I did was under the watchful eye of my son.

A person tends to act differently when they know they are being watched, and I was no different. I soon found myself slowing down my speech, smiling more often, being more patient, and exaggerating all of my facial expressions and hand gestures. I started directing other family members to adjust their behaviors and their speech patterns also. I changed. Other family members changed. We learned to communicate differently, more openly. Once I figured out how to open that door (by learning how to communicate his way), I could help him. I finally was able to open that darn door. It was then up to Matt to find the courage to step across the threshold, and he did.

This one action, stepping through the door, didn't happen overnight. It took years of baby steps and continues even now, over twenty years later. Matt can interact with family and friends fairly well, a bit differently than other people and more cautiously, but he can interact. He can read emotions and body language, though sometimes he can't quite understand the more complex ones like loneliness, or the more subtle ones like someone not feeling well. He still watches, still practices, and still takes mental notes on how to proceed in any given situation. This is where hope emerges for a life of independence. It is the need to be more like others that drives him, and it is his courage that puts one foot in front of the other as he steps through door after door.

Most of us take for granted the simple ability to communicate with others, to socialize, to bring our ability to understand body language clues and society norms into our everyday interactions. With an autistic child, we find we need to look at all of it differently. We need to learn new ways to communicate and keep our minds open for new revelations about interactions and body language. It all starts when we as parents and caregivers learn to take notes on the behaviors and body language of our autistic child.

Take some time today, right now, and make your own covert observations. In doing so, you too will be hearing the tapping at the door. Once you figure out how to open that door (by learning how to really communicate and interact), then you too will witness something truly amazing—the indomitable courage of your child stepping across the threshold into the realm of the unknown, simply to be with you.

THEORY OF MIND
JUST WHOSE MIND ARE WE
REFERRING TO HERE?

THEORY OF MIND...I know you've heard of it. You probably
looked it up to see what it meant and came across the term
"mind-blindness" and found it used as a way to explain autism.
So many professionals use this in a detrimental, formal way to
characterize individuals on the spectrum and suggests, whether
intended or not, that autistic individuals are incomplete in their
humanness. Let me ask you this: do you agree?

Theory of mind, the ability to relate to another's thoughts and
emotions. A very fancy way of declaring empathy as it relates to
social communication. Can you place yourself in another person's
shoes to understand why they act the way they do—do you feel
their pain? Take a look around you. How many neurotypical people do you know that could care less about the unemployed, the
homeless, the sick, or the elderly? Neurotypical people are not
always empathetic, or our society would be a much better place.
And yet, when discussing theory of mind, neurotypical individuals are assumed to possess such a depth of empathy as to declare
it as part of our humanness. As such, suggesting that autistic peo-

ple do not have theory of mind is, in essence, stating in a subtle way that having autism makes one somehow less than human. Researchers conclude a seeming lack of ability to empathize as a result of data obtained from the infamous Sally-Ann test.

If you scan the research, you will find many references to the Sally-Ann test. Sometimes this is given as a set of pictures, and sometimes it is shown as a video. Here's the situation presented to the child being tested:

Sally and Ann are in a room with a box and a basket on a table. Sally is shown putting her marble in the box and then leaves the room. Ann, having seen Sally put the marble in the box, walks over, retrieves the marble out of the box, and hides it in the basket. Then Sally returns. She wants her marble. Where will she go to retrieve her marble, the box or the basket?

Seems fairly simple, but then in autism, nothing is that simple. In asking the child "Where will Sally look?" they are asking the child to empathize with Sally, put themselves in Sally's shoes. But in autism, some things are just not that black and white. We have to ask ourselves, what is the priority of the child being tested? The child, if they are anything like my son Matt, is always concerned about being right. As a young child, Matt had to get an A in every class. A simple B caused terrible pain and meltdowns. He just couldn't think of himself as being less than anyone else. A B made him feel...imperfect. He still has this type of thinking, over twenty years later, and he still strives to do his absolute best. Yet underneath it all still remains a fear of failure, a possibility of imperfection.

Now take this into account when grading a Sally-Ann test. It's a test, and as such, he would want to be correct. He knows where the marble is, and he knows that Sally does not know where it is. He is being asked to choose between saying Sally will look in the box, where he knows the marble is not (Sally would be wrong), and saying she should look in the basket, where he knows it to be (Sally would be right). Since they are asking him to be Sally and he would not want to be wrong, he will choose the basket. Basically he is confronted with a dilemma: either pick where the marble is not (box) or where the marble is (basket). This has nothing to do with an inability to empathize and everything to do with self-worth. If they are empathizing with Sally, then they don't want her to be wrong—it's an awful feeling to be wrong. Maybe they just want her to find her marble so she won't be upset...

When a child states through whatever preferred form of communication, whether it's verbally or in gesture, that the marble is in the basket, the researchers assume this child could not put themselves in Sally's shoes and, by deduction, must lack a theory of mind. The researchers missed an important component to this type of test. They forgot to put themselves in the shoes of the individual they were testing. So I have to ask, just whose mind are we really talking about here in regard to lacking empathy?

I see this as a perfect example of how autism myths arise and are then justified to society—with the end result portraying being autistic as somehow less human. Isn't it interesting that only neurotypical people declare autism as somehow less than human? Shouldn't we ask an autistic person what it is like and whether they feel empathy? There are plenty to ask. But instead, society as a whole ignores the plethora of information available from actual autistic people, preferring to listen to people who apparently have trouble communicating with actual autistic adults. Does this even make sense to one person? In articles written by autistic people, they are quick to say that they would not choose to be "cured" of their autism "disorder" because to them, their autism is an integral part of who they are. And yes, they do have empathy. But it shouldn't matter anyway because all they really want is to be viewed as just as important to society as everybody else.

So why must we have a view of autism that constantly focuses only on ways in which to fix it instead of also including ways in which to promote cooperative communication? Shouldn't neurotypicals (such as myself) be as willing to learn the various forms of communication an autistic individual (such as my son) chooses to use at least as much as the autistic individual is required to learn to communicate in the ways in which we choose? And if communication really were a two-way street between neuro-typicals and autistics, then wouldn't researchers be aware of the empathy present in the autistic without such meaningless tests as the Sally-Ann?

It is my own personal opinion that for someone to state that an autistic person "lacks empathy" is to declare ignorance of the reality of autism. If you are reading this, then you are most likely a neurotypical parent of an autistic child. Think about how you would characterize autism in your own words based upon the 24/7 interaction and experience you have with an individual on the spectrum. After taking into account all that you know—and remember, *you* are the expert on your autistic child—then how would you respond to someone declaring (in scientific journals no less) that your child has no theory of mind?

My response to these researchers and professionals would be "Have you people no theory of mind yourselves?" After all, if they are unable to put themselves in the shoes of an autistic person, then they themselves lack theory of mind. If they cannot explain a situation involving an autistic person, then they must be suffering from mind-blindness. And if they cannot see that these children are overwhelmed by sensory issues, communication differences, fear of failure, and bombarded by social cues being forced upon them, then perhaps they lack real empathy.

So I ask you, just whose mind is really deficient in the ability to put themselves in another person's shoes?

OH, THE JOYS
OF POTTY TRAINING!

I DIDN'T THINK we would ever get out of the diaper stage. How do you potty train an autistic child? First, they have to learn control, and second, they have to learn to clean themselves. It's nasty business for adults. Think of how nasty it must be for someone with an acute sense of smell and touch. Matt was in diapers for years. We tried everything to get him to control his bladder. Nothing seemed to work. He was either five or six years old and diapers didn't fit well anymore. Training pants were always wet. Even the pre-school was tired of changing him. Our nerves were shot. We just didn't know how to proceed.

One summer afternoon, I was out on the deck watching Matt in the kiddy pool. He even had to wear a diaper in the pool because of lack of control. His disposable training pants were saturated from pool water, and it was time for him to get out. It practically fell off as he stood up. I grabbed the dissolving clump before it could hit the deck. Nude and loving it, Matt ran around the deck in the hot sun. Tom had just come out the door, and we were laughing at Matt's obvious joy of being naked. Christopher came out to see what all the laughter was about.

I'm not sure who had the idea first. Was it Christopher or Tom? Anyway, the next thing I knew, both were standing at the edge of the deck and peeing into the yard. Matt was fascinated. Matt has always been fascinated by water—sounds of water, the flow of water, the feel of water. Here were both his brother and his daddy making beautiful arcs of water—Matt stood there in complete awe. He was hooked almost immediately. He ran to the edge and stuck his belly out as far as it could go, pushing his back with his hands, and began to pee. I stood there stunned. I would have been mad if it weren't for the fact that it worked—and they all seemed to be having so much fun!

Every day after that event, Matt would stop what he was doing and run outside to pee. Clothes were easy to remove, and the training pants were finally becoming useful. Matt loved the pool and spent most days naked as jaybird, splashing around and jumping out to pee off the deck. We lived in the country, no one was around to see, and I couldn't see any harm in it. When we had my stepkids, Jacob and Sarah, for the weekends, Jacob would join in, and Sarah and I would retreat to the house. Sarah, who was only seven years old, was very jealous, and to tell the truth, so was I.

It was this particular summer that our cat had kittens. They had a nice little shed just off the deck where they stayed with the momma cat. At six weeks of age, we put an ad in the paper and started receiving inquiries. A woman and her two children came by to see the cute kittens. They were petting each one, trying to decide which kitten to take, when out came Matt, stark naked, and jumped in the pool. I called for Tom, and before Tom could get out the door, Matt had decided he needed to pee. He slipped past Tom, ran to the edge, and let it fly. The woman mumbled something like, "We need to think about it," as she quickly hustled her children toward the driveway to escape. I found this to be extremely funny and started laughing. Tom laughed, and Matt, hearing the joyous sound, laughed too. His behavior had just been reinforced. He was controlling his bladder in the privacy of our yard. What harm could it do?

Then sometime in the middle of summer, we decided to go to the local flea market. We gathered up the kids and Matt's changing bag and headed out. Each child was looking at items on nearby tables, staying close enough so we could keep track. Matt stayed right with us. Tom and I were discussing an item we had found when I heard *the* sound. Matt had dropped his pants and was peeing right there, in the middle of a crowd! What could we do? He was in full stream. We looked at each other for only a moment. I moved to block the view, standing on one side, and Tom calmly moved to stand on the opposite side. Christopher and Jacob walked over and began to giggle, but taking a cue from us, moved to block the view. Sarah wandered over and, seeing what was happening, just smiled and joined the ring. We managed to block any and all view of Matt or the stream. The entire crew worked like a well-oiled machine and, without words, came together to protect Matt. No one in the crowd seemed to notice. We decided to leave before anyone could say anything to counteract that assessment.

It took all summer to get Matt to pee in the toilet. It took all summer to make him stop peeing off the deck (and he never again let loose in public). But we did it, and Matt was on his way to self-control.

Bowel movements were something quite different. First, Matt couldn't figure out why a part of his body kept coming out. What was that nasty stuff? Sitting him on the toilet and waiting and waiting and taking him off the toilet and cleaning him up seemed to take an hour each time. Matt would watch the water swirl with each flush. Where did that nasty stuff go?

He evidently needed to explore this phenomenon. One day I found him in the bathroom, stuffing plastic links into the toilet. Plastic links are those brightly colored blocks of various shapes that link together to form long lines. Matt was trying to find out just how deep the hole in the toilet bowl went. He would shove the entire linked chain as hard as he could then add a new link. We tried to remove them, but each pull resulted in a simple disconnect of a link. The blocks that were in the hole were wedged in tight. Tom finally had to take a blow torch to the toilet to melt them free.

Of course, this was followed by clogging the toilet with toilet paper—an entire roll. Matt was learning to clean himself, but instead of using just enough, he became fascinated with the dissolving properties of the paper and just couldn't stop. Another plumbing nightmare (and more would come). We became experts at plunging.

Ah yes, potty training. We were both experienced parents when it came to potty training a child. But we were amateurs when it came to potty training an autistic child. We needed creativity, a great deal more patience, and a sense of humor to pull through.

The best part—if there can be such a thing?—it's finally over!

ENJOYING THE MAGIC
OF CHRISTMAS

As CHRISTMAS APPROACHES, I can't help but reflect on the years past and how my son Matt has changed in his own way to embrace the spirit of the season. Matt is almost twenty-six years old, so there's plenty to reflect upon. As I thought about all of our unique experiences, I wondered, "Do other parents of autistic children have this much fun?"

I use the word "fun" because looking at it from my point of view it would all make such a great movie, a comedy, I think, about learning the true meaning of Christmas. Don't get me wrong, there were a few years with too much family drama. Some were budget-breaking extravaganzas, while others were completed on a shoestring financially. Some were tearful due to overwhelming joy and others tearful because they were absolutely heart-wrenching. Yet all, every single one, ended with the warmth of a love-filled home, smiles on children's faces, full bellies, and plenty of unforgettable (and sometimes pretty hilarious) memories.

We always went on a drive to see Christmas lights and decorations on or near Christmas Eve, and we always waited to put the toys and gifts under the tree until after the kids were asleep. This was a challenge as every year for ten years Matt would camp out in the hallway with his pillow, blanket, and fan (he has slept with a humming fan next to his head all his life) to await the arrival of Santa (maybe catch a glimpse), and we had to traverse this blockade without waking him. It was a two-person job, a team effort, just to get the packages from point A (bedroom closet) to point B (under the tree.) Matt never knew, never awoke even once, and it kept the magic of Christmas alive, and the illusion of presents just suddenly appearing under the tree safe for another season.

There was the year of my divorce (my boys were very young) where I had nothing to give my children, no money to buy gifts and no tree decorated and blinking. A few days before Christmas, friends and family got together and delivered a small decorated tree, supplied gifts for my children, and took us into their home for a holiday feast. Just days before I had been caught crying by Matt. He responded by crawling into my lap, putting his hand on my face, and saying "momma" for the very first time. It turned out to be one of the best Christmases ever for me.

There was the first Christmas after autism set in when Matt loved the boxes more than the toys that came in them. There were several where he fought Santa tooth and nail at the mall, and another where the one toy he wanted was the one toy we searched for in store after store for weeks to no avail and had to leave a note under the tree that promised one would arrive soon. The Christmases after he could write were much better because we encouraged him to write to Santa (you know, that bearded guy he fought tooth and nail just a year before). The letters gave us insight to what he really longed for and sent us on a mission to obtain said items early in the season to make sure a note would not have to go under the tree ever again. Matt asked for a wide variety of items over the years: building blocks and Lego kits, Ninja Turtles, Ghostbusters, *Jurassic Park* vehicles, *Toy Story* action figures, *Thomas the Train* VCR tapes and train accessories, space shuttle models, airplane models, a Big Wheel, a bike, *Home Alone* tapes and art supplies, books, clothes (as a teenager he became aware of his appearance and actually wanted clothes!), and sports paraphernalia for Virginia Tech. Take a look at that list again. Nothing in it says autism…nothing.

Church plays and concerts were met with tantrums and meltdowns. Matt hated the loudness of the music and, although fascinated by the plays, did not wish to partake as one of the shepherds. Instead, Matt crawled under the pews or walked the periphery or explored any region of the church he could get away with. This meant I was constantly looking for Matt while trying to watch our other children perform. And there were times when I had to miss something—a line, a song, a part of my other kids' holiday, to run after or console a weeping Matt. But children of all ages act out at times or are afraid and must be consoled. I would wager that most parents at one time or another miss their other children's stuff too. Autism doesn't cause the problems. Childhood does.

And while visiting Santa was traumatic as a small child, he finally did grow a desire to talk to the big guy in the red suit, and it evolved almost overnight into a must-do ritual. Did it really matter that he was now ten to twelve years old and twice the height of the other children in line? Did it matter that he would only stand next to Santa and talk, not sit on his lap? It never fazed Santa, it never fazed Matt, and it never fazed us.

Then one year it happened—Matt no longer wanted to see Santa. He had become skeptical of the magic tale, and he needed something more. It was finally *time*. We all know it will happen, and we all know we have to eventually break the news to our kids, but how you do it matters. It matters a lot. Breaking the news of the childhood lie was something I had thought about for years, literally. When it came time to sit him down, I was ready. I told him that little children believe in a Santa Clause because it is magical and fun. I told him that as a child becomes an adult, they know something is amiss. This is because they get smarter. I told him that adults are Santa, and when they become adults, it is their job to keep the magic a secret and be the Santa for others. Matt especially liked this idea. He would be the secret Santa and keep the magic alive. He took this responsibility to heart.

Every year since our talk, Matt has been the essence of the Christmas spirit. He hunts for items for each family member and wraps them and puts them under the tree. Matt even buys for himself. He wraps it up and puts a tag on it—*To Matt from Santa*—and on Christmas morning, he opens the gift that he himself wrapped and is wonderfully surprised and excited to find exactly what he wanted. His joy at watching Charlie Brown and Snoopy, the Grinch and Rudolph is contagious as well as his excitement at decorating a tree, stringing lights, and wrapping gifts. Matt lights up our home and our hearts. Our other children are all grown up and moved away into their own homes and are creating their own season of magic. Yet even with our children grown and our house mostly empty, we still have plenty of the Christmas spirit lighting every dark crack and crevice. Matt reminds us daily that it is love that matters most, not the gifts or twinkling lights or Christmas songs, but the deep desire to give the gifts, wanting to display the lights, and to sing the songs that makes it all so magical. Autism does not prevent the desire, and it does not prevent the love from being felt. Autism is just the surface. What is inside each of us is what matters, autistic or not. For my husband and me, Matt makes Christmas, Christmas.

I know it sounds too warm and fuzzy to some of you. I can assure you it was not always this way. We felt the aloofness of extended family members, the constant veil of stress, and jumped the hurdles that appeared almost daily from out of nowhere. But that was *then*. Something changed along the way, and it wasn't just Matt. It was me too. I am now the one who rides the waves of autism with him taking away from each experience the comedic factor and laughing away the conformist part of me that used to think everything had to be just so perfect. I understand now that life really is what we make of it—should Christmas be any different? Enjoy the quirks, survive the stress, and be ready to look back and hopefully laugh a little. Think of the stories you could tell!

Matt just finished wrapping another gift he bought for himself and placed it beneath the tree. I can't wait to see his surprised and joyful expression when he opens that same gift on Christmas morning! It's Christmas—autism style.

BEAUTY OF WATER

WATER, AN EXCELLENT tool in the desensitization of an autistic child. It can change temperature, be filled with bubbles, and create sounds (bubbling, flowing in creeks and rivers, the "plunking" sound of rocks tossed into it). The level can be adjusted up (swimming) or down (a glass full). Items tossed into the water sink or float. Sound changes underwater. All fascinating qualities to explore for any young curious child, but especially fascinating to my autistic child.

Matt knew the sound of running water. It drew him like a duck to, well…water. He loved it. Give him a glass of water and sit back—the experiments were about to begin. Small toys, like Lego blocks, would be dropped into the glass. Squinting, his head turned to the side, he would watch the item fall to the bottom out of the container from the corners of his eyes. Sometimes Matt, only three years old, would climb onto the kitchen counter, get a glass himself, fill it, and drop a toy, "plunk," into the water.

He also loved trajectories, and water was a great tool in manipulating trajectories. An item dropped into a container of water didn't always sink straight down. Sometimes it swirled and danced in circles as it made its way to the bottom. Sometimes the object wouldn't sink at all but instead floated along the surface. These were discoveries made through his own curiosity, and I encouraged the experimentation.

The sound of water delighted him so much that he would come running whenever someone turned on the water, be it in a sink or a tub or a hose. He would then watch fascinated as the water flowed and could not resist plunging his hands in to feel the power of the stream. If the water was running in the tub, he would hurriedly remove his clothing, a flurry of movement that left behind items of clothing from his room to the bathroom. I would have to catch him before he hit the tub to slow him down. He had no concerns over slippery wet floors, but I did.

Matt didn't appear to feel pain during this stage, and he could have injured himself without our knowledge if we weren't careful.

Bubbles were an added bonus, but not required. As he got a little older, he would first find a toy, or several toys, to take with him to the tub and have them ready to grab for bath time. Matt was always eager for bath time as more experiments could be conducted and repeatedly retested. Toys were submerged and watched intently as bubbles of air scrambled to the surface. He studied the above-water phenomena first; floating, sinking, small bubbles or large, the varying sounds of water displacement each time a toy was dropped. After his repeated above-water observations, he would make underwater observations. He hated water on his face, but allowed his ears to dip beneath the surface. Experiments in the physics of sound waves came next as he lay on his back, listening.

Sound changes underwater. The sounds of voices are muffled, and annoying background sounds are eliminated. Matt could focus on the physics of water just as he had focused on the physics of gravity with his toys outside. He would study the problem through observation then experiment. He would lie in the tub, the water creeping over him until it reached his ears. Slowly, he would submerge them. Most above water sounds decreased, and some sounds, I am sure, were eliminated altogether. The lowering of the noise level was always a welcome relief for him.

Many autistic children have sensory overload. Everything comes into the brain at the same level, no background noise, all forefront noise. I can't imagine the stress. How terrible to have to deal with so much sound! Water provided a much-desired filter. If he could only see underwater, his observations would be complete. He needed a face mask and snorkel.

Summer brought heat and humidity and the purchase of a small pool, the kind adults buy to soak their feet. Matt could lay in it for almost an hour before emerging as a prune. When we purchased a face mask and a snorkel, his life took a new turn—

the underwater experience! After placing the face mask just so and tightening the rubber headband, he slowly bent toward the surface. His face would immediately pop back up wearing a grin as if to say, "No leaks! Yep, this will work just fine."

He spent as much time peering underwater as he could stand before rising up to take a breath. Learning to use the snorkel was next. He practiced breathing in and out in the safety of the air before testing it under the water. Smiling again as if to say, "Yep, this will work too."

He became a pool junky. He would come running, jump in, splash around a bit, then after a few moments of simply splashing would stop and get down to business. He brought toys with him, items that would sink, so he could follow their trail as they cut through the water to rest on the bottom. Such a little scientist! Hmm...time for a bigger pool.

We purchased one of those large pools that require a filter and separate lining. The blue of the water called out on those hot summer days, and the kids all headed for the ladder. The other kids would jump from the ladder and splash around, followed by a brief dive beneath the surface. They battled each other with smacks of their palms on the surface, aiming the splash toward their intended victim. Matt could only play this game if his face mask was on, but he would try to play. As the other children, tired of the water games, crawled out shivering, Matt was left with the pool to himself. Now the interesting stuff could begin. More room to move, less sound and activity. This was what really thrilled him, as now he could explore the bottom without legs everywhere. He stayed just enough above the water to watch the item in his hand be released then softly sank to witness the trajectory of the item to the bottom.

His love of lines and motion were satiated in water. He could see the patterns without squinting or turning his head. He could watch from a full-frontal point of view and actually see the trail as it emerged. The trails meandered, swishing left or right, creating beautiful patterns in the filtered light. I know, because my own curiosity led me to watch underwater as his experiments took place. Having no mask or snorkel forced me to the surface for air, but I would repeatedly go under until I saw what he saw.

Over the years the other kids became interested in retrieving items from the bottom of a pool. Matt loved this new game. Hotel pools were the best—plenty of room, various levels of depth. The race to find the item evolved into a family game using a coin. Toss a coin and retrieve it from the bottom. Of course, Matt had to slip beneath the surface to watch the trajectory and motion of the coin as it sank before anyone could attempt retrieval, but other than that he played the game with all of us. A new way to interact as a family was born.

I knew from my observations of my son that Matt was a deep thinker with an analytical mind. Just the sheer amount of time he devoted to inquiry was astounding, and yet many people just couldn't see what I saw. Although I had been told my son was unable to have independent thought, I could not agree. I saw a mind craving answers, a curiosity insatiable. To me, Matt's brain seemed to be working overtime. In taking it upon myself to see what he saw, I discovered more about the world through his eyes.

They say that beauty is in the eye of the beholder. To Matt, a meandering line through the water backlit by the sun was a beautiful thing to behold. I couldn't agree more.

A WONDERFUL LIE

IT HAD BEEN twelve years and never a lie, not one. How many parents can say that about their child? As Dr. House (from the TV show) would say, "Everybody lies." Autistic children were at one time thought incapable of such stealth and critical thought. I found that was not the truth. Sometimes it takes a bit longer to learn how, but everybody lies, even those with autism. It took twelve years before I actually caught my autistic son, Matt, in a lie.

Prior to the big event—the telling of a simple lie—I had assumed Matt was incapable of such a dastardly deed. Up to this point in time, if something happened and it needed explaining, Matt was the person to go to because he always stated the facts, and just the facts, with no embellishments at all. Whenever I would get after my oldest son, Christopher (the usual suspect in these matters), the excuses and explanations were usually some wild tale, which, of course, brought about immediate suspicion. At these times all I had to do was turn to Matt and ask him if the tale was true and Matt would give me the facts. Matt never showed signs of being uncomfortable in this position. To him, the world was either black or white, and the current tale Christopher wove was either true or false.

"Um, I think Chris did it," came out very matter-of-fact. He would then provide the details, and the jig was up. My oldest would reply indignantly, "You always believe him over me!" Christopher was then usually…"grounded." Disgusted by the whole situation, Christopher would stomp to his room. I'm sure he felt betrayed, ratted out by his little brother. It was like watching a scene from some old gangster movie. The glare from Christopher could have easily been interpreted as, "Look you, you squealed to the coppers, you dirty rat. Someday you're gonna get yours."

The world of black and white changed to gray with Matt's first lie. I was walking past Matt's room and noticed something odd. Matt was playing quietly on the floor, and next to him was an old WWII army helmet, which belonged to my husband, Tom. The item was kept in his closet in our bedroom. I stopped and looked at Matt and wondered, did Matt actually go in our bedroom and rummage around in our closet? Matt looked up at me, waiting for me to say something. Since I always said something to him as I passed his room, it was no surprise to see this expectant look on his face.

"Did you take this?" I asked, walking over to pick up the helmet. The look on his face darkened.

"Um, no," he said softly.

I tried again. "Matt, how did Daddy's helmet get in here?" I waited for the details in black and white as usual.

Matt looked right at me and said, "I think Chris did it."

Somewhere down the hall a frustrated "Ha!" arose followed by a hardy laugh from Christopher. "I did not! Matt! You little stinker!"

Of course I knew Christopher didn't do it. Matt was the one that loved the army gear. He had developed a love for anything army over the previous few years: combat video games, WWII books and films, and he even drew army tanks and battle scenes in his art (I'm talking reams of paper depicting every type of battle imaginable!). I had no doubt as to who took the helmet. It was

Matt who liked to wear the helmet, the flak jacket, the coat, and carry a gun (a Nurf blaster). Tom often retrieved these items from his closet just so Matt could pretend to be a soldier.

I knew at once that Matt had just lied. *Matt…just…lied!* The enormity of this began to register. Matt had just lied. He really lied! I had to scramble to think of what to do next. I knew that telling him he was bad for having lied to me would immediately result in tears and confusion because Matt has always thought of himself as perfect. To even imply he wasn't was asking for trouble. His self-esteem was the foundation that determined whether any type of learning could proceed. Low esteem and Matt would withdraw, preventing any learning to take place. High self-esteem and he was proud to show you what he knew, and he was open to learning new things. I was constantly building his self-esteem. Matt knew he was different, and he fought it daily, wanting to be perfect. For example, if I told him he did a great job, he would simply agree with a yes. If I praised him for completing a task, he would smile and agree with me—"Yep, I'm the greatest." When I would praise him and tell him he was smart, it would elicit a "Yes, I am."

Unfortunately, telling him that he lied would signify imperfection…a flaw. Recognition of a flaw was a trigger for a meltdown. Yet I knew the terrible deed had to be done. I had to tell him lying was bad.

Let's just say he didn't take it well. The tears and anger surfaced immediately, and the anger was pointed directly at me. "No, Momma, you lie!"

Wow! I didn't see that one coming. What great deflection! It was so unexpected that it caught me completely off guard.

"I didn't lie, when did I lie?" I stammered.

I had immediately been put on the defensive by my twelve-year-old son. He proceeded to unveil a long list of situations and events as examples of my lying prowess: I said we would go a certain place and we hadn't, I said I would buy him a certain toy and I hadn't. The list kept going. My god, this kid had been keeping score for a very long time! I was flustered. He had artfully turned the conversation around and made me the bad guy—and I felt it. In order to get the focus back on him, I knew I had to first own up to all my misgivings, admit I had indeed "lied." I then apologized for my lies and asked his forgiveness. That settled him down to a point where we could now at least discuss the situation calmly.

We talked a long while. In the end, he understood that he had lied and needed to tell the truth. He gave me the detailed rundown, the black and white, of the entire sequence from his room to Tom's closet and back to his room to retrieve the helmet. I was actually relieved to know he would still do that. Once he was calm, new learning could take place. He learned the closet was off limits and that he could not take things from our room without asking. He learned lying was a bad idea and being caught in a lie was very painful indeed.

I also was open to learning new things. I learned that I needed to keep my promises better. If I told him we would go somewhere, then we would. I also learned that Matt was just as capable as any other child to skew the lines of truth, and another misconception about autism went the way of the dodo. Communication took a new direction for both of us.

I never again asked Matt to squeal on his big brother. Matt's earlier expression of "I think it was Chris" underwent a metamorphosis to "Christopher did it!" A private family joke. A Frisbee on the roof? Christopher did it. Toilet stopped up? Christopher did it. Global warming? Yep, Christopher did it. Christopher took it all in stride and enjoyed these tales of dastardly deeds and superhuman evildoings and would eagerly claim to be the mastermind for even the wildest of tales. Matt would laugh at all the tall tales and actually took pride in revealing the ones he himself had done, making sure we knew the real circumstances in black and white. "No, I put the Frisbee on the roof." Matt would argue.

"No, I did it!" Christopher would shoot back, bringing another round of laughter between them. This interplay of fantasy and fact actually brought more than one bonus—it allowed Matt to see that he could tell the truth without getting into trouble and that his imagination was limitless. It also opened up another door to communication and interaction for Matt with each member of his family. This meant that socialization skills, the next step in communication, were also enhanced.

This was sixteen years ago when Matt was only twelve years old. Autism awareness did not exist on any meaningful level back then. No one knew an autistic child could do such wonderful things as imaginative play, or feel any remorse or guilt or empathy. Therefore each tiny glimmer of these things was a lightbulb moment for me and my family.

Dr. House was right. Everybody lies. Even the tiniest of white lies is still a lie. The discovery of a simple lie, while not a big deal normally (after all, parents deal with it all the time), was an earth-shaking moment for me. This simple act coming from my young autistic son confirmed what I had long suspected—he did "feel," he did "think," he did have an "imagination." Remember, this happened a long time ago, and back then it was widely thought that autistic individuals were incapable of such human characteristics. So when it happened, it was a really big deal. I was proud of Matt's first lie, just like I was with his first step and his first word. Truth be told, I even did a little dance when he wasn't looking, releasing my inner joy in a moment of immense satisfaction for having never believed the autism dogma of the time. My son was different—yes, wonderfully, uniquely so—but he was not less.

The telling of a lie, a very human trait, was a moment to celebrate a newfound inner peace of what it actually meant to be autistic. My eyes opened. The world seemed brighter somehow. And yet, the only thing that had changed was that Matt had told a lie. A wonderful little lie.

CRITICAL THINKING
AS SIMPLE AS READING A MAP

AT THE AGE of four and a half years old, my son was still not doing age-appropriate behaviors. When we took him back to the Kluge Center for Children for his last follow-up evaluation, they ran a battery of cognitive tests. The results were still grim and not only showed he had a bimodal IQ (certain skills were higher than average, and certain skills were very low) but showed he was incapable of independent thought. I immediately took issue with the way the tests were done. How could they possibly say such a thing? Didn't they see the wonderful little boy I saw? This was in 1990, and autism was rare and thought to result in a robot-like child without the ability to learn. It wasn't just the doctors and the therapists. It was also the way special education teachers thought of the disorder. Matt was already in preschool, a special education preschool, where he spent most of his day hiding under tables or pacing in the back of the classroom. No one saw any point in teaching him because, well, he couldn't learn anyway. How does one change that pattern of thought?

The way I saw it, Matt's sensory processing difficulties were not taken into consideration with the types of tests they did. So while the curious behaviors of autism took center stage, the child underneath was all but forgotten. I finally had my fill of testing when Matt failed a test designed to evaluate his level of critical thinking. To this day I take issue with how it was evaluated. Consider this method for yourself.

Matt was shown a box with a lock on it and given a key. The idea was to see if he possessed critical thinking skills and independent thought. Evidently, the average child can do this even if they have never encountered a lock before. I'm skeptical of this assumption. The lock and key test was sprung on him suddenly. The occupational therapist gave him a key and set the locked box in front of him. She then began timing him with a stopwatch. He had never even seen a lock or a key, and he had no curiosity about what was in the box. After several minutes, she secretively marked her grade sheet.

"Did he fail?" I asked.

"Well, he didn't even attempt to open the box and never showed any curiosity," she stated back.

"But Matt can do that trick," I countered. "Give me the key."

She politely handed me the key, placating the hysterical parent before her.

"Matt, watch this!" I said directly to Matt as I sat on the floor beside him.

Matt watched as I put the key in the hole, turned, opened the lock, opened the latch, and open the box. I picked up his toy car he had brought with him and placed it in the box. I shut the lid, flipped down the latch, and put the lock back on.

"Listen," I said as I clamped the lockdown until it produced an audible "click."

Matt watched the whole sequence. His car was now in that box, and the box was locked. I handed him the key. Matt put the key in the hole, turned it, opened and removed the lock, flipped the latch, and opened the box to reveal his beloved possession still intact. A wonderful smile lit up his face. He was genuinely relieved and now fascinated by the lock and key.

"See?" I said to the therapist. She looked at me as if I had just spit on her.

"Well, he was not able to do it without you showing him," she replied.

She never changed her grade sheet, and Matt failed the test. In his medical record, it was recorded that my son was unable to think critically and had no measurable independent thought capabilities.

That last visit really was the last visit as far as follow-up evaluations went. Their methods were questionable and the results highly inaccurate. Basically it had really gotten under my skin and I refused to accept their conclusions. The problem was how do I prove them wrong? So while I was unwilling to accept that Matt lacked thinking skills, I had no way to show them that he did have those skills. His autism behaviors, the outward signs of autism, always took center stage. Testing had shown there was no one present underneath. My beautiful son was considered to be mentally incapable of learning...just a robot. He was in a special education preschool class, but he spent most of his time under a table or pacing at the back of the room...and the only person it bothered was me.

As the years crept by, Matt continued to show me skill after skill, but nothing I could declare as an ability to think critically (where a problem is analyzed, worked through, a solution tested and evaluated, leading to logical thought and self-guided learning). I watched him as he played, and although I was sure he was thinking through what he was seeing and evaluating what he was hearing, I knew that just synthesizing sensory information was not considered true critical thinking. That all changed with the introduction of the most unlikely educational tool, the video game.

Matt grew up with the release of video games to mainstream America. He learned to play because he was fascinated by the movements on the screen, which he could control. He mastered such favorites as Sonic the Hedgehog and others and would spend hours playing. I remember when the video game for Jurassic Park came out—it was a "must" purchase for Matt as the movie had been one of his favorites. The game promised lots of dinosaurs and jungles and various weapons of destruction—what's not to love?

I learned to play the video game too as a way to interact with him, and I even made it to the end of the game eventually, but I didn't play very often. Matt, on the other hand, was a Jurassic Park ninja at the age of seven. He played daily and for hours at a stretch. He had to win—just had to! He competed with his steps-iblings, Jacob and Sarah, and with Tom and me, and he won 99 percent of the time, but not against his older brother, Christopher. When those two played, it could be best described as a clash of the titans. Speed clicking the controller, thumbs flying, bodies in motion, eyes glued to the screen—a true battle between video ninjas. It was because his older brother was so good at it that Matt made it his mission to learn all the secret codes that would garner him more hidden points. He learned to decipher the simple schematics of the island map, which kept him headed in the right direction toward winning the game.

The map had a *You are here* and showed the various locations of battles and treasures and how to get to them. A map was a way to get from point A to point B, and this revelation led to an interest in all maps: geographical, road, world maps, etc. This skill bled over into his drawings, and teachers began to sit up and take notice. Although he was nonverbal, he could name the capitals, draw a state's shape, write the sequence of route numbers from one place to another—his knowledge was showing up in his art. Deciphering the symbols in the key of a map provided clues on where the next turn would be on any given road, where the highest elevation was in the state, or when we traveled across a border to another state. Reading a map was like seeing the future, as he could see ahead to what would come next, removing some of the mystery and fear of the unknown. I didn't realize the importance of maps until he made one of his very own, but I didn't see the importance of it right away because my attention was on something else...my garden.

I was outside designing and planting new flowerbeds and deep into creating a new walking path. Matt was outside with me. Matt couldn't care less about gardening, but he was fond of making ramps in the newly tilled soil for the pleasure of launching one of his small toy trucks into the air. The ramp was continually modified at ever-steeper angles in order to send his toy in ever higher trajectories...it's a Matt thing. He was fascinated by trajectories at that age, and many a toy was launched off the deck, the kitchen countertop, or any high surface so that he could watch the object out the corners of his eyes as the toy flew in various shaped arcs (depending on their weight) until it crash-landed. His joy in this activity was obvious as he would jump and twirl with glee after every successful launch. It was also very routine for him to carry paper and pencil with him at all times in case the need to draw these trajectories and crashes overcame him. And so it was that particular day that Matt had a small toy truck he was launching off the dirt ramps and paper and pencil by his side as I worked in the garden...just another "normal" day.

A few days later, as we were having lunch, Matt brought me a picture. The paper had a newly drawn picture that I couldn't quite decipher: a confusing set of lines, an X, and what appeared to be a truck. The paper had a bit of dirt on it. Not sure what I was seeing, I simply told him how nice it was and gave it back. He handed it back to me, but this time he pointed at the X and exclaimed, "My truck." Thinking he wanted me to acknowledge his scribble of a truck, I simply said, "It's a nice truck." Evidently my reply was not what he wanted, and he pointed again, "Truck."

Okay, what is it about this truck? I stared at it, trying to make sense of his picture. There were straight lines and a few crossed lines and the X and a simple sketch of a truck. I just wasn't seeing what he had intended me to see and sadly handed it back to him. Frustrated with me, he took back his artwork, turned, and left. We spent the next several hours in the house, and the normal sounds of him playing his Jurassic Park video game filled the air. A few hours later, it suddenly occurred to me that the house was too quiet—the sounds of dinosaurs screaming had ceased. I went to look in on Matt. There he sat in his room, his video game on pause, drawing the animation of the Jurassic Park Island displayed on the screen.

The following day he brought me another picture and again pointed to the X. "My truck," he exclaimed again. Again I looked it over, and again I did not see what he needed me to see. But Matt never gave up. Day after day he brought me a picture of lines, an X, and a truck. Try as I might, I couldn't figure out what he was trying to tell me. Several days later, I took him back outside to play while I again headed for the garden. When Matt realized we were headed outside, he ran back to his room to get his picture. His excitement caught my attention, and I watched as he stopped at the door, looked at his paper, and then took very deliberate steps across the deck and into the yard. I wish I had continued to watch as he took each step according to plan, but I missed it. I had assumed he was just playing some odd Matt-type game, and instead of watching him, I went to the garden.

Before I started digging, I looked over at Matt. He had also come to the garden. Paper in hand, he dropped to his knees and began to dig. Matt didn't like to dig, so this was something new. Now he had my attention. I watched as he turned over the dirt by the handfuls until finally his hands brought up a toy truck. The lightbulb finally glowed above my head as I exclaimed aloud, "Oh, I get it!"

Matt's picture was a map. I asked Matt if I could see his picture again, and I finally saw what he wanted me to see. He had buried his truck in the garden and had drawn a map to its location. The confusing set of lines had actually been a fairly accurate diagram of the deck and lawn. The truck was buried treasure, buried underground, and the X—well, the X marked the spot.

A big smile shone brightly on his face as he happily showed me his map. As I looked deeper at each line, I noticed he had added a "You are here" sign on the line that represented the back door. I understood. Matt must have added it after I had trouble deciphering the last map. Determined to make me understand, he had gone back to his game, restudied the island map, and tried to match the details of that map to his own. Now having successfully communicated to me what he wanted me to know, he stood triumphant, truck in one hand and dirt-smudged map in the other, and marched back toward the house with his head held high.

I stood there amazed at what just transpired. My son had just demonstrated critical thinking. He had used the island map on his video game as a template for making his own map. He then tested the map and, seeing that it confused me, had adjusted the map to more accurately depict the starting point. Matt had thought through a problem, analyzed it, and tested it—and repeated the stages as he sought new information on how to communicate his map to me. These are the same steps that demonstrate the use of critical thinking skills. And while this may seem like common knowledge now, back in the early 1990s when autism was rare, this skill was considered something new. His use of critical thinking, using something as simple as a map, showed me there was much more to my son than the unique behaviors associated with his autism. The assumption that he would never be able to learn was finally debunked. The best part was watching his determination to communicate with me. He had given me clues, tried to tell me the best way he knew how (with pictures), and remained steadfast in his mission to communicate his newfound skill with me. It was obvious—finally—that his mind was so very capable of deep, independent thought.

So here was the fork in the road, and now it was up to me to decide which way we would go. One direction led toward a special education classroom and basic skills learning and the other toward challenging his mind and his abilities to think. I gathered up all my courage and decided to take the new, harder path, the one without road signs, the one that would push him to learn and think. I decided to attempt something not done before by anyone here in southwest Virginia—mainstream an autistic child into a regular education classroom. There would no longer be a straight line from point A to point B. This different road was certain to be very confusing and possibly impossible to traverse, but I was willing to attempt it. I wasn't scared. I had an ace in the hole, you see. I had a map. I knew my son could give me the clues to what he was capable of along the way, and just like a map to his future, I knew if I got stumped on which way to turn or the number of steps to take to get to the next destination, it would be okay, because Matt didn't just draw the map, he taught me how to read it.

We changed our path that year—it was 1993. We started to transition him from a contained special-education class to a regular class in 1994–1995, and he was fully mainstreamed into the third grade in 1996. Although Matt is moderate/severely autistic and mostly nonverbal, he continued in a regular classroom (with the help of his aide) throughout the remainder of his school years, graduating in 2005...with honors...as a National Honor Society member...and number four in his class. A road we took because he made a great map and taught me how to read it.

GROUNDED!

DOESN'T IT SOMETIMES seem like every parent you come across thinks they have perfect, angelic children? No such luck here. I have real ones. My children got into trouble, did things they knew to be wrong, pushed the envelope of parental sanity, and paid the ultimate price—they were grounded.

My oldest, Christopher, could push the limits better than anyone. He was (and still is) an extremely bright boy. His teachers even suggested he was gifted and should be accelerated to the next grade. Since social ability was a big factor in our lives, I told him the decision was his—he chose to stay with his friends. The problem was that he was bored enough to plan outrageous stunts and intelligent enough to pull them off. Of course, he didn't have a naive mother either and was caught red-handed more than you would think. As Christopher got older and more cunning, Matt got older and more admiring. Christopher was his brother, and no matter what, Matt always had his back.

Matt was learning some important lessons during this time: how to dress, how to form a sentence, and personal hygiene. I was teaching him these things, but observing his brother do these things gave him the added desire to learn. If his brother could do it, then he wanted to learn to do it too. Things I didn't teach him, but he learned quite readily anyway—like how to play video games and use a computer—he learned mostly from his brother. He wanted posters on his walls and even started listening to music.

Matt observed how Christopher interacted with family and friends and animals. He watched him fix his own meals and buy his own toys. Matt watched him admiringly at wrestling matches, and met his friends and his girlfriends. Of course, the love went both ways. "No one messes with Matt" was Christopher's credo. That sentiment was reciprocated as Matt had his brother's back too.

Matt was around eight years old when he first stepped in to defend his brother. I had grounded Christopher for something—I don't recall what (there were so many). Matt stormed out of his room and marched up to me.

"Christopher is *not* grounded!"

I looked at him. "Yes, he is, Matt."

"No, you don't grounded my brother!" he snapped back.

Imagine, this quiet child who rarely ever raises his voice, much less speak, arguing with me. He turned and marched to his brother's room. Afraid to actually go in, he stood at the doorway and peered in. Was his brother okay? Was he hurt? No one would hurt his brother! He stood there a moment as if trying to decide if he should go in, block the doorway, or let me have it again. He decided to let me have it again. The only way to calm Matt down was to apologize for having said that word. I am sure Christopher was secretly smiling.

It was unlike any argument I had ever had. Shocked for only a moment, I started to smile—my little boy was connected enough to another human being to fight for him. Were autistic children supposed to be capable of that? It's hard to argue when you're happy. I couldn't contain my joy, which confused Matt. I laughed, Tom laughed, and snickers were heard from the bad boy's room. Matt calmed down. Anger dissipated. Life was good.

This became a normal routine. I would ground Christopher, and Matt would read me the riot act. Laughter would end it all. It was all just too cool! Matt could hunt me down, look directly at me for seconds longer than normal, and stand his ground on an issue he felt passionate about. He could defend another human being. He could clearly state his objection and did not accept compromise. This was the most obvious example of independent thought. He was thinking, feeling, and expressing his thoughts, and they were expressed with such emotion! How could this not be viewed as cool?

Over the years, Matt became more insistent that I stop using that word. Matt was about fifteen years old when he really let me have it. Yep, Christopher was grounded again. Matt was furious and in no uncertain terms informed me that the word "grounded" was a bad word, a dirty word, on par with a four-letter word and I was to never use that word again, not even in jest or casual conversation. Not ever!

To this day that word is not allowed in our home. Matt must have related the word to the pain he saw in his brother's eyes, or the anger on his face, or worse yet, imperfection. Whatever emotion it connected to, it is as strong a connection now as when he first made it. We still abide by his wishes, not willing to upset him over such a trivial thing—the use of one little word. That particular word evolved over the years to stand for something else—a new meaning—a symbol for Matt's own growth toward independent thought and emotions. In my mind, it stands for independence.

While writing this, I asked Matt if he still hated the "G" word. His brow deepened, an angry look swept over his face as he told me, "Yes!"

"Why do you hate it so much?" I asked.

He gave me his most serious face, eyes staring directly at me as he raised his arm and pointed upward, "Because it will anger the gods!"

So there you have it. I am probably breaking Matt's rule just writing about it (I feel so sneaky, almost criminal!). No other word has ever elicited a response that comes near to that of the "G" word. The only one that comes close was the "no" word (which initiated meltdowns in his early years). Yet even a word that could ramp up a meltdown could never compare to the emotion elicited by the "G" word. I can't remember the last time I even said it out loud—except maybe in jest. Do I dare say it again? "Grounded."

CARTOONS RULE

CARTOONS BRING JOY, laughter, inspire imagination, and are a great learning tool. Bet you didn't see that last one coming.

Right now Matt is watching Bugs Bunny, the new DVD he just bought. The DVD is a collection of the classics, and Matt grew up on the classics. Bugs Bunny and all his friends, the familiar theme songs and character voices—what a blast from the past. Matt has been steadily laughing now for five minutes straight. I take a moment to listen—ah, Road Runner and Wiley Coyote. No wonder he's laughing so hard.

Cartoons have always been something I enjoy, and I started my kids out early on the antics of such characters as Tom and Jerry, Scooby-do, the Flintstones (I know every episode by heart), and of course, Bugs Bunny. Matt has found cartoons, especially these silly ones from the past, to be the most enjoyable too. He has openly laughed while watching since he was just a toddler. There were times in the car that Matt would burst out laughing and we would all look at each other quizzically. "What's so funny?" we wondered. I had to wait until he could speak to find out the answer to that question—Road Runner and Wiley Coyote, Bugs Bunny or some other cartoon. Yep, all those times he would burst out laughing, Matt had actually been replaying the cartoons in his head, watching these reruns in his mind and laughing at all the right moments. If you asked him "What's so funny?" he could describe the entire scene to you, complete with any road signs poor Road Runner had to read, or Bugs Bunny or Elmer Fudd held in their hands.

Holidays and birthdays always brought VCR tapes of classic cartoons from the grandparents. Matt literally wore out each tape (and two VCRs). Each replay brought hardy laughter and memorized speech, which was fine with me. I know, I know. I should have modified his behavior—according to all those experts who have no autistic child of their own. According to them, I was supposed to try and curb his desire for routines and "strange" behaviors. But I must confess I liked it (gasp!). I loved hearing the joy. I loved seeing the smile. Why in the world would I break his heart over something as trivial as watching cartoons? So I let Matt enjoy his cartoons and his movies over and over (and over and over) until the tape or the VCR just couldn't play anymore. And Matt stayed happy and openly displayed this most precious of emotions. Did it ever do any real harm? Well, I guess if you counted how many people thought they would lose their mind after hearing the same cartoon eight to ten times in a row—but heck, they're family, so they just accepted it and suffered.

I have another confession. I still love cartoons. I haven't watched any of the newer ones. They are not the same. The plots are too serious, or they are just not goofy enough to suit my sense of humor. Matt understands—he likes goofy too.

So as I sit in the den and listen to his laughter—yep, still going on—I think about how much joy this child carries with him every day. He laughs so readily; he smiles and jokes so easily. Hearing the sounds of joy fill my house, I am glad that I never took away his desire to replay tapes. I survived, my family survived, and Matt grew up with laughter and joy. In the end, the only thing that really matters is that my son is happy.

From all indications, he is enjoying his new DVD immensely. I sit and ponder on the teaching value of such silly animations. The facial expressions are really obvious for each character—you definitely know what they are thinking.

A Daffy Duck with a face full of buck-shot from Elmer clearly displays disgust, loathing, and shock. A Road Runner looking at a bowl of seed tainted with explosives clearly shows intelligence and a "yeah, right..."

Matt laughs at these expressions because he can read them clearly. He could watch the facial expressions of animated characters long before he could stand to look at a human face. He was safe with the animations—and he learned facial expressions relate to human emotions. He also picked up a wonderful sense of humor and an easy laugh—two very endearing traits.

So did they teach Matt anything? Of course! Every exposure to cartoons taught something. Children learn through interacting with their environment. What type of environment we choose to expose them to is up to us. An autistic child learns the same way in this regard—their environment is everything. Watching the classics (cartoons)? Well, they're really just another minor player in the entire scheme of things, but vastly important to Matt experiencing joy on command. Having a bad day? Turn on the cartoons and watch the bad times slip away.

As I finish writing, I hear the whistling sound of a bomb dropping on Wiley Coyote and a very hardy laugh burst from Matt. Yep, cartoons rule! To this day, whenever I hear a cartoon on, I know the laughs are not far behind. It remains music to my ears.

HOW ART TRANSFORMED
AN AUTISTIC MIND

WHEN MATT, WAS a little over year old, he would hold up a ball in one hand, extend his arm, and turn it this way and that, looking at it from all angles. That was when I knew that Matt would someday be an artist. What I did not know was that he would soon be autistic as well. When the initial symptoms of autism arose, it seemed to put Matt's mind on hold, and in many ways regress. Sensations from light and sound to simple textures became uncomfortable. He had to deal with the onslaught of his environment, and it was overwhelming. These were unsure times—would my son be tortured this way his entire life? Would he ever be able to communicate with me?

I look back now and am amazed at how fast Matt learned to deal with these intensified stimuli. In dealing with such a change in his perceived environment, Matt went through a period of adjustment—the classic autism behaviors arose. He had regressed so much that I wondered if he had lost his artistic eye. Had it been lost, or had art simply taken a backseat to the emergence of his autism? It wasn't until several years later that I noticed his eye for perspective and talent toward perceptual-conceptual art was still intact.

Matt began to draw as all children do with scribbles using a crayon or pencil. He drew simple lines on a page at various angles without pattern or reason—what I called his "primitive art." That changed the day I drew a picture of a train for my oldest son, Christopher. Matt watched in fascination from a short distance away as I sketched a train. I was teaching Christopher to draw and talked to him about lines and perspective and copying from a simple picture. I showed him how to create simple details. Soon my simple lines on a page became something recognizable—a locomotive. Christopher began to draw his own version, copying from a picture in a book and adding small details. Matt had watched the whole lesson, and even though he was only three years old, he was hooked—drawing fascinated him.

From that day on, Matt would bring me a paper and pencil and force it into my hand as a signal to me it was time to draw a train. This became another daily routine—that is until I decided to change things up a bit. Again, Matt brought me the paper and pencil, and I promptly sat down on the floor with him as expected. This time, however, I placed Matt in my lap and put the pencil in his hand. I covered his hand with mine, and together we drew a simple train. Matt was nervous, and his grip on the pencil waivered, but I held firm, and we continued on until a simple locomotive appeared on the page.

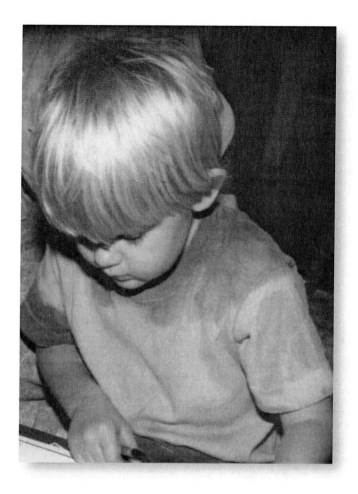

I let his hand go. Matt put his new drawing on the floor and started to copy it himself, just as his brother had done. His lines were barely visible as he lightly scribbled across the page, trying desperately to create an image. The lines were somewhat chaotic, but they soon merged to form a somewhat recognizable image—a locomotive.

From then on, Matt drew daily. Beauty is in the eye of the beholder, and while primitive in its form, his pictures were beautiful to me. I watched him evolve to create new patterns and lines on page after page and often wondered if these patterns actually meant something. Could they be revealing his thoughts? Still unable to speak, I understood that Matt could be trying to communicate thought through his art. With this in mind, I examined each piece of his primitive art with deep interest. What was the meaning behind the shapes and the lines? One of his early drawings—a set of three V-shaped lines in row after row—was something he would draw almost every day. What were the three Vs?

Then one day while riding in the car, I glanced back to see Matt staring upward out the window. In a moment of curiosity, I leaned back and looked up. At first I didn't notice anything of interest. Refusing to give up, I kept my gaze upward, and that's when it hit me. I finally saw what was so fascinating to my son—power lines. It was one of those a-ha moments that I will never forget. The large power lines that traversed the mountains near our home created a pattern of long, straight lines. Each power pole had a set of three V-shaped connections. Matt had been drawing the power lines. I learned an important lesson that day. There really were messages in his artwork. The most important is that my son had thoughts of his own and was not incapable of independent thought or feelings. The professionals were wrong about that dismal prediction.

Something deeper was also ignited in moving pencil across paper—a fascination with the skillfulness of drawing and a desire to be capable of creating by hand what he saw in his mind. Matt still asked, in his own nonverbal way, for me to draw for him. It wasn't what I was drawing, but the act of drawing that was tugging on his soul. Matt wanted to create. As he watched my hand draw line after line, his hands would flap faster and faster. Obviously, Matt was getting more excited as the picture emerged from the previously blank page. It didn't take long for the fascination to turn into an obsession—Matt now *needed* me to draw for him every day, over and over. Don't get me wrong, I didn't mind drawing—I love to sketch—but the amount of time I was spending repeatedly drawing one train after another was preventing me from doing other needed tasks. I wanted Matt to draw for me, but he was very frustrated by his own work—it didn't look like what he wanted it to look like.

Finally one day, on the spur of the moment, I changed our routine…again. I put the paper over a picture of a train on the cover of one of his train books, picked him up and put him in my lap, placed the pencil in his hand, and covered his hand with my own. Together we traced the train. I picked up another sheet of paper, and we traced the train again. This time his hand had a firmer grasp, and he directed the pencil instead of me. Soon a picture emerged of the train from the book cover—a bit shaky and not very pretty, but still it was clearly the same train and Matt had drawn it. I didn't know it at the time, but on that day I had given my son a skill that changed his whole life.

Tracing gave him a newfound pleasure in art. Now he could create a drawing, and it would look as it should. Drawing was *not* just a pastime; it was a *necessity*. Unfortunately, he couldn't trace while at preschool and had to draw freehand. Each day he brought home assignment papers from school, I would immediately turn them over to look on the back of each page. There I would find the most interesting drawings. Unable to trace, Matt had to recall his favorite items from memory. He would draw what he saw in his mind's eye. These were of course very childlike drawings, not up to the standards of perfection he expected from those that he traced.

In order to correct this perceived "flaw," Matt had to teach himself how to draw freehand. Matt would sit in his room and draw the same picture over and over. The first few were traced from a picture of his choice, and the next would be drawn freehand. He never erased. Each time a line was drawn at the wrong angle or too long, he would crumble the entire sheet into a ball and toss it away. He had to have perfection. His hands would draw slowly at first, getting each detail just right. Then he would repeat the process over and over until his hands could fly across the page and draw the most intricate of pictures in less than five minutes, without tracing.

This isn't all that unusual if you think about it. Lots of people train their hands—crocheting, making pottery, driving a stick shift. Practicing over and over allows one to perform a function without looking. Matt's love was drawing, and he trained his hands to draw without thinking about how his hands moved. This allowed him to draw anytime and anywhere without having any of his beloved train books in front of him. He began taking paper and pencil with him where ever we went—always ready to draw if the need overtook him. Drawing calmed his mind, allowed him to focus on the minute details of various objects, and decreased his fear of new surroundings and sounds. He used his art to communicate as well, telling me what he needed and what he was thinking. Matt had found a way to make peace with a chaotic world.

As Matt got older, his interest veered more toward animation. The cartoons he watched became a daily ritual, and the characters became his imaginary friends. He would repeat the spoken lines of each character and add a few responses from himself. His new friends began to show up in his art. Again, Matt would practice drawing each facet, his hands moving slowly at first. He practiced drawing just eyes, then just facial expressions, and then body gestures. Page after page of practice allowed him to then combine these pieces to show any situation and every type of movement. Each new drawing became more and more detailed. Between the ages of twelve and sixteen, Matt learned to draw himself and began putting himself into his drawings along with his cartoon friends.

As part of learning to draw, Matt was also learning new social skills. He used his animated self to interact with his animated friends, converse, and display both sad times and good. Watching him interact with animated characters concerned me at first—was this new behavior a good thing or a bad thing? I chose to think of it as a good thing—after all, he was learning to interact, even if it was not with real people. I'm glad I decided to just let it flow out of him this way because I soon realized his ability to interact with real, live people was improving dramatically. Matt had used the safety of his art to practice social skills and emotion. After getting comfortable with his animated friends, he could now test his newfound skills on family members and schoolmates. Matt found a way to communicate without an overwhelming fear of the unknown.

Matt still takes paper and pencils with him wherever we go. Most times it is like taking a safety blanket and the items are never used. Sometimes he sees something and just needs to draw it—like the various street signs, or the beach at Hatteras, but these drawings are for later use in the stories he writes. Matt realized his animations needed dialogue—after all, comic books and cartoons each have a story line. So Matt not only draws, he also writes. Where in earlier years he could only communicate through his body language, he now can communicate through speech, the written word, emotion, body language, and various forms of art. His stories revolve around his own life, historical events, and places he has both visited and places he has yet to see. Art has transformed his mind. The great strides that he has achieved are all a result of his attention to detail, hours upon hours of drawing, and in the evolution of drawing objects to drawing situations and stories. Autism has finally taken a back-seat to who he really is—an artist.

If I could pinpoint one pivotal moment in Matt's life that changed his whole world and changed the path of his life, it would have to be the day that I put Matt in my lap, placed a pencil in his hand, placed my hand gently over his, and we began to trace. I didn't know it at the time, but that one act—that simple fifteen minutes of attention—gave Matt the one thing he needed to transform his entire life, a way to express himself through his art.

MELTDOWNS
IN SEARCH OF THE TRIGGER

HOW DO YOU deal with defiance? It's hard enough for a parent to deal with defiance from any child, but what about from an autistic child? I can look back and see that it all could have been handled so much better if I had understood the triggers that initiated the meltdowns. One specific trigger always resulted in a battle of wills and physical strength. If I had only known then what I know now, those battles would have fallen away at a much earlier age.

Although I learned early that Matt had a prescribed formula in the progression toward a meltdown, it took me years to discover their root cause. For those of you who don't know what a meltdown is, I would describe it as an escalation of defiance to the degree of def-con 4 (possibly 5) as compared to a typical temper tantrum, which I would rate as only capable of reaching def-con 2. Regrettably, the cause was not discovered until years later, after Matt had already been through numerous high-level meltdowns. Imagine my shame when I discovered that I had unknowingly triggered the worst of them.

"How?" you ask. I told Matt "No!" The trigger to a meltdown turned out to be one simple, and completely avoidable, word.

When he was still nonverbal (prior to the age of five), defiance was expressed in various behaviors—crying, screaming, hitting, biting, or my all-time favorite, the full-body lockdown. Child-proof locks on cabinets didn't prevent him from opening the cabinet door under the kitchen sink, and the latch on the back door didn't prevent him from escaping to the yard, then to the road, and down to the creek. Considering the dangers a child is surrounded by on a daily basis, you can understand why I used the word "no" a lot.

I didn't realize back then that Matt's comprehension of the word "no" meant something more painful than a simple veto. The word "no" meant "rejection" and suggested disapproval of him to his very core. I now realize Matt has hated this word since even before he could actually say it. When he was young, I attributed his emotional reaction as pretty typical for a preschool-age child—maybe a bit on the exaggerated side, but I was a fairly new mom—what did I know? I didn't see the pain, not really see it, until he was between eight to ten years old. Prior to understanding the cause of his meltdowns, I had unlocked the pattern of behaviors indicating one was imminent and could at least prepare myself in advance for the ensuing battle.

The sequence began with a very stern "No!" from me. This was met with a show of defiance from Matt. Upset, crying, and angry he would make it clear he did not approve of my rebuff and was determined to continue whatever it was he was doing. Pushing limits, that's what I thought he was doing. So of course, I said "no" again, even more forcefully than the first. My second use of the word only made matters worse. It lit the fuse for a meltdown. Swinging fists and kicking legs was usually his choice at home. However, in public it was a full-body lockdown.

In a full-body lockdown, Matt would drop to the floor and stiffen all his limbs. It was his way of saying, "I'm not leaving."

Picking him up was difficult, but not impossible. After forcibly standing him partway up, either my husband or me would swing him over a shoulder and carry him out as if being rescued from a fire. You can bet there were plenty of stares from passersby—and they were not kind stares, if you get my drift.

If we were home, Matt preferred to fight. To prevent him from injuring himself or others, I would have to physically contain his movements. First, I would pull Matt to the floor with me from behind so that he sat in my lap. Then I hugged him—tight. My arms wrapped his arms, my legs wrapped his legs, and still he was able to head-butt me a few times. Once in my arms, Matt would struggle mightily to free himself until finally he just broke down. Exhausted physically, Matt would suddenly go limp. Then the angry cries, which had been filling the air from the onset, changed to gut-wrenching sobs. As I sat on the floor holding him, I would rock us back and forth and speak softly in his ear. I knew by the anguished cries and the limpness of his body that the battle was over.

Nothing in this world has the power to rip my soul to shreds like Matt crying. His cries are no ordinary cries. They come from somewhere deep inside him, and when they surface, they release all the anguish of his frustration and despair. They are so sorrowful that if I hear his cries for longer than a few minutes, I will cry as well.

Before I let him go, Matt would always shift his body so he could look at my face to make sure that I was again smiling. Smiles meant everything was going to be okay. It took hours sometimes to calm him down to the point that he could go on to play again. A meltdown left us both physically and emotionally spent. The worst part was thinking we would have to go through it again someday, as there always seemed to be a next time.

Although I knew the routine and what to expect, I couldn't connect the dots between his extreme reactions and a simple reprimand. I often wondered about how it would be in the future.

Would I have to physically contain him as a grown man? Was that even possible? I knew the day would soon arrive when Matt would get the best of me, and knowing Matt, he would not be able to handle the guilt of hurting me or anyone else if something happened. Still, I couldn't figure it out.

I wish I could say that my superhuman powers of deduction found the trigger, but that would be a fallacy. Matt actually told me, "No more 'no!' No more 'no!' Please!" in a voice wracked with both pain and sorrow. How would you interpret that? He could mean he doesn't want me to say he can't do something, or he could mean, quite literally, he doesn't want me to say the word "no." In autism, most things are meant literally. The next time he was reprimanded for something, I avoided the "no" word, and although Matt showed disappointment, and some confusion, there was no meltdown. I was in shock. Could it really be that simple?

For all those years I had not taken him literally. All those forcefully stated "no's," all those battles that didn't need to occur. How many times did Matt fight to preserve himself and force the "anger" in my voice to go away? I had raised him on smiles and laughter. I had coaxed him to interact by showing him smiles and lessening fear. When he saw my face and heard my voice as I reprimanded him, it was as if his safety net had vanished and he was falling. Meltdowns released frustration and anger but also were an indicator of fear. Meltdowns were the only way he knew to fight back.

Thankfully, I eventually became aware of the power of the word "no." Things didn't escalate if I used another word or phrase. Saying "Not now, Matt" or "We can't right now" was handled much more smoothly. Although I kept expecting the situation to rise to def-con 4, it rarely rose above def-con 3. When it did escalate, his screams would intensify, and I would instantly become aware that I had said the word "no" again.

I stopped using the forceful "no" years and years ago. There have been no meltdowns. I have said "no" in fun and in phrases like "no way!" to help desensitize him to the word, and he now handles hearing the offending word quite well. That's probably because he always examines my face to see if I am smiling. Knowing this, I have reserved any stern looks to times when I absolutely have to use them.

Autistic children live with fear—lots and lots of fear. We work every day to make the world feel a bit safer for them, but still fear lurks just beneath the surface. Fear accounts for many autistic behaviors. Is it such a leap to think that fear also underlies the meltdown? I realized that Matt, for all his accomplishments and progress, still struggles beneath the surface to cope. He handles all the ups and downs so well that I forget sometimes that fear is hiding just beneath the surface. An angry face or a sternly uttered word from another person and Matt could be pushed toward a possible meltdown. Even now at twenty-five years old, it is still possible—though I hope the likelihood has diminished. If it did happen again, I am confident I could intervene and stop it before it escalates, but what happens when I am not there anymore?

This is why I write—to let others know what autism is and to encourage other parents to look for deeper meaning behind each behavior, even meltdowns. If you are struggling with meltdowns from your own child, I highly recommend hunting for the trigger. All children with autism are different, but they do have a common thread…an underlying fear. Remember that for every action (trigger), there is an equal and opposite reaction (meltdown). I am convinced that for autism this is true. Every outward behavior has an underlying and purely logical reason. As parents and caregivers, isn't it up to us to try to understand them just as much as they are trying to understand us?

If I only knew two decades ago what I know now…

SPEECH
A BATTLE AGAINST TIME

MATT'S FIRST WORD was "kitty," and it was uttered before autism arrived. After autism Matt was nonverbal and remained nonverbal for several years. After his diagnosis, I set him up to receive speech therapy. This entailed a meeting with school officials as Matt was also to receive home-bound preschool services. At that meeting, the speech therapist informed me that he would see Matt in his office once a week.

Let's back up a minute. Learning to speak has an expiration date. Time is limited. The section of the brain that gets wired for speech is fairly active—until around age five, after which the connections for the ability to speak slows down, becoming nonexistent. In other words, if he didn't learn to speak by age five, then chances were pretty good that he would never speak. Matt was three years old. We had two years to get him to speak, *two years!* To me, two years was right around the corner…once a week speech therapy would just not cut it, simple as that.

Matt was diagnosed when autism was still rare and teachers, professionals, friends, and relatives had never heard of the disorder. Matt was entering a school system that had never dealt with an autistic child. Matt was the groundbreaker, I was the force, and every child to come after would be judged by what we accomplished. I was fighting for Matt, yes, but I was also fighting for any child that would come after. This was weight I carried into that first meeting for services—Matt's first IEP.

Upon hearing the "once a week" suggestion, I politely told Mr. Speech Therapist that once a week was not enough. He needed it daily (always start with more than you will accept). He countered two. I pushed for three. By this time voices were being raised, and one of those voices was mine. I was speaking for my child—who could not. The therapist actually countered my request with…and I kid you not…that Matt didn't need speech that often because he didn't speak. I'll let that sink in a minute.

Well, as you can imagine, that got me to my feet. I slammed my hands down on the table (causing all the other members of the committee to flinch and jump back in their seats). I explained to this man the science of speech, and that his role here was to help my son achieve speech before the expiration date. Matt received speech therapy three times a week.

The story doesn't end there.

Trying to get Matt to speak was an everyday, every-waking-hour task. One of my son's favorite things was water, and I must have said the word to him thousands of times as he played in the tub, the pool, experimented with bubbles, etc. At Matt's first speech session, the therapist (still a bit chilly from our last encounter) spent the time trying to get Matt to sit in a chair. Matt didn't sit in chairs, he sat behind them, or used them to stand on, but not sit. Mr. Speech Therapist was spending all of his energy on an unrelated behavior with the clock ticking on verbal communication.

The therapist spent so much focus on the "getting seated" agenda that he missed Matt's first word. Matt climbed onto the chair, tapped his finger on the picture on the wall of cows by a stream, and very clearly said "wa." I was in awe. The therapist tuned me out when I tried to explain what had just occurred. I went home, called the school board, and fired my therapist, and requested a new one (best move *ever!*). The next week, we met Debbie, his new speech therapist.

I was ready to fight again when we approached the school where Debbie worked. I found her office, and she came to the door to greet us (us!). Here was an elegant woman, wearing a dress with a flowing skirt and high-heeled shoes, very professional looking, and she ignored me, kicked off her shoes, and sat on the floor, getting down to Matt's level. I was impressed. She began giving him various toys and speaking softly only to him. I sat quietly in a chair just inside the door and watched this interaction for twenty minutes. She looked at him, trying to gain eye contact. She asked him questions and provided answers (demonstrating how to reply).

After months of visits, she had gained his trust. Matt began to speak—simple words, but words all the same. Matt was four years old, almost five. Matt continued to see Debbie for the rest of his school years, and their bond was so tight that when he was asked to nominate his favorite teacher for "Who's Who" (honor students get to do that), he chose Debbie. Speech therapists do not usually get such recognition, and her genuine surprise and joy was captured for all to see in the town newspaper.

During this same period, my first husband and I divorced (not so unusual if you look at the statistics for divorce among couples with a disabled child). One night, just days before Christmas (and three weeks before Matt's fifth birthday), I was sitting in the living room, tears on my face as I thought about my circumstances. Matt heard me crying and crawled into my lap. I hugged him tight as the tears continued to fall. Matt looked at my face, placed his palm on my cheek, and softly said "Mama" for the first time.

Speech, it has a window of opportunity, and it must be addressed as the number one goal for an autistic child...because hearing your child say "Mama" is just too important to let it pass by without a fight.

TELLING TRUTH FROM FICTION

MATT IS A History Channel fanatic. He is also fascinated with disasters. What could be better than a disaster show on the History Channel? Unfortunately, Matt believes everything he sees on the History Channel—all of those animations and graphics and recreations. After all, if it is on the History Channel, it must be true. Of course, the narrative of the show describes events and what is possible and discusses both the pros and cons using various experts. But Matt doesn't seem to listen to everything they say—nope, just the actual disaster parts. "The Mayan Prophecies" and "Nostradamus Effect" are the two shows I'm really concerned with as Matt has watched both of these repeatedly. Both discuss the Mayan calendar and the prediction for the end of the world.

A person learns by various types of stimuli and usually has one type that is better for them than the others. I'm talking about visual (what you see), auditory (what you hear), and tactile (what you feel with your hands). For some, watching another perform a task is the best, where others want the explanation of how to do it and still others don't quite get it unless they put their own hands on it and do the task themselves. All have their good qualities, and all contribute to the learning process. Each person knows which is best for them.

Matt has always been more of a visual learner—watching others, observing phenomena, deciphering schematics and maps. Of course he has learned many things through both tactile and auditory methods also, but he is definitely more visual. For him, his autism has made his senses acute. That means certain things feel weird, and sounds can be painful; even bright lights are avoided. His sense of hearing is very fine-tuned, and not in a good way. When he was young, his mind would pick and choose what auditory stimuli were good and which stimuli were bad. For example, the sound of a lawn mower made him cringe, forcing him to cover his ears. Fire alarms during a fire drill at school just about tore him to pieces. No one in the house could ever raise their voice in anger or yell (parent behavior modification resulted from that one!). Dogs barking, vacuum cleaners running, and trucks downshifting on our road all brought his hands to his ears to lessen the pain. No wonder autism is a communication disorder—we are a species that relies heavily on sound to communicate, and sound was not welcome in his world. So it should not surprise me that he had developed selective hearing.

Over the years, he learned to listen better. He learned that if I was talking to him, he needed to look at me. I had to make sure my voice was calm and soft. He learned to connect the visual (my face) with the auditory (my voice). I thought we were past the stage of learning to listen until we took him to the movie *2012*.

On the way home, Matt seemed on edge. Something was wrong. Shouldn't he be talking excitedly about the movie he had just seen? I turned to him and asked, "You do know that the movie was just fiction, right? It wasn't real, Matt."

"Yes, it is!" he countered.

This caught me off guard. What? Where did he get that idea? "It's true," he continued. "I saw it on the History Channel!"

He was referring to the show "The Mayan Prophecies" about the world coming to an end in the year 2012—because the

Mayan calendar said so! He obviously had not actually listened to the narrative of the show, which describes what some people think, what the possibilities were, and the science that shows it to be just a legend.

"The History Channel was only showing what some people think," I argued back.

His face became red with anger. "It is true! It's on the Mayan calendar."

We argued all the way home, but I could not convince him that he was not going to die on December 21, 2012. He had been living with the fear of the world ending, of him dying, knowing there was no safe place on the earth to hide. It made me sick to think of him feeling his life would soon be over, that he had absolutely no control, that death awaited him in 2012.

When we arrived home, I talked to him again about the History Channel and told him to really listen to what they said.

"You need to just trust me on this—just listen to all of what they say, Matt."

Today the DVD came out for the movie 2012, and I took him to get it. We hurried home so he could see his new movie before we had to leave for class. I watched it with him, and we talked a little, mostly about the Yellowstone Super Volcano (will we ever be able to visit there? Not if he thinks it could erupt again.) I didn't argue and didn't make any remarks about it being a Hollywood flick. I just wanted to enjoy our time together.

As the final scene ended and the credits started to roll, Matt turned to me and said in his happy, on-top-of-the-world voice, "This is just fiction, it isn't real."

Cool! That was unexpected. He must have watched "The Mayan Prophecies" again and actually listened to the debate.

"That's right, Matt," I said smiling.

Wow! He had made a judgment based on the auditory alone. He actually allowed his ears to take precedence over his eyes, at least for this one time. I wanted to jump up and dance, dance,

dance! But I sat there calmly, allowing him to take full credit for a job well done.

"You like disaster movies a lot, don't you?" I chided.

Matt then began to list his favorite disaster movies, adding at the end that they were all just fiction.

Yep, Matt feels secure again. He knows that his life still has endless possibilities and decades more time. He knows movies are just Hollywood and the History Channel is more than just cool graphics as he's getting better with that "selective hearing" thing. It was wonderful to see that he could think critically if given all the information, and it's good to know that he now actively seeks all the information by using all his senses, not just his visual pathway.

With a mostly nonverbal autistic child, I often don't realize what stimuli are being processed, what information makes it in, and what information is filtered out because his speech is so rare. I have to rely on other clues to find out what exactly Matt learns. Now that I am aware of the auditory funnel, I can help him out by repeating certain points a speaker makes—whether on the television, the radio, or in person—so that Matt is sure to pick up on it.

Learning fact from fiction requires critical thinking skills. Critical thinking skills require full sensory participation. Not exactly an easy thing to do for someone like my son who has sensory-processing difficulties.

T-BALL AND M&Ms

THE WARM BREEZES and smell of fresh-cut grass each spring brought with it the sign-up for spring sports. My oldest, Christopher, had decided to play baseball. We practiced batting with him in the front yard as Matt circled the perimeter, watching. To look at him, you would think he was oblivious to the world around him, but we knew better. If you glanced his way on occasion, you could catch his quick scan of the situation. There was, after all, a ball that would take flight, and we knew how much he loved a good trajectory.

On the day of the sign-up, as we sat on one of the picnic table benches near the door at the elementary school awaiting our turn to complete the sign-in process, we were taken by surprise when Matt revealed he also wanted to play ball. It wasn't a clear "Mom, I want to play." It was more of a change in his facial expressions, his eyes darting from his big brother to me then back to his brother. A combination of gestures, simple words, and longing looks suggested Matt really, really wanted to play ball too. I didn't know what to do. Christopher and Matt are two and a half years apart in age, and Matt was just a little guy, not old enough to play baseball.

I was trying to explain this to Matt when a tall young man walked up. He had witnessed my failing attempts to console my son and invited Matt to join his new T-ball team. His name was Dennis. Dennis didn't know Matt. No one at Christopher's school did because Matt attended a different school, out of this district, to receive special services for his disability. I explained this to Dennis.

"Would Matt be allowed to play for this school?" Dennis asked. "Can he run?"

I nodded my head.

"Then he can play!"

Thus began the T-ball years.

STEP 1: TEACH MATT HOW TO HIT.

Silly parents that we are, we assumed that what we needed to teach Matt was how to hit the ball. We had Matt stand, bat in hand, and tossed him a ball. As the ball left my husband's hand, Matt turned his head as far away as possible so he could view the incoming trajectory out of the corner of his eye, squinting. Smack!

Cool! Matt can hit. We were ready for T-ball! We were so naive.

We felt sure Matt would hit the ball and run like the wind at his first game. He had been marking days off the calendar all week and was jumping, literally, with excitement come the big day. He ran toward the ball field, proudly wearing his game shirt. As he awaited his turn, he would march back and forth, keeping a good distance between his teammates and himself. Sometimes he walked in small circles, talking to himself and darting his eyes toward the T when someone would step up to bat.

We watched from the bleachers as each player stood at home plate and tried to hit the ball off the T. We were anxious to see Matt play, to be involved in a *team* sport, something no one thought he would ever do.

Finally, it was Matt's turn at bat. He swung...and hit the T. He swung again, swish, nothing but air. Swung again, hitting the T and a small portion of the ball, just enough to knock it off the stand. It began to roll forward, and yells of "run" arose from the crowd. Matt ran to first base, turned, and to everyone's surprise, ran right back to home plate, where he was pronounced "out!" Oops...we forgot to teach Matt how to run the bases!

STEP 2: TEACH MATT TO HOW TO RUN THE BASES.

You hit the ball, and then you run here, then here, then here, and then home. The look on his face said it all: "Are you nuts?"

Second attempt. "The bat hits the ball, the ball goes flying and you run from base to base and try to beat the ball to home plate." The look on his face? "My parents are loons."

Third attempt. We need some bases. We grabbed some typing paper, numbered them in large black numbers—1, 2, 3, and one for "HOME." Then we placed each sheet on the ground in a diamond, each resting on the grass where a base should be. We had Matt stand at home plate, gave him a bat, and pitched a ball toward him. Smack! To the calls of "drop the bat" and "run to no. 1," Matt dropped the bat and ran to number 1 then turned and ran back to "HOME."

This would not be easy. We took him by the hand and walked him from base to base against his will. This will never work! You can't just pull him from base to base until he gets it. His will was probably stronger than mine, so we could do this all day, and in the end, he still would not run the bases. Suddenly, I got an idea, M&Ms.

Sure enough, Matt would run from base to base to receive a candy reward. M&Ms were his favorite candy, especially the color green. Standing at second base with a handful of M&Ms brought about the desired behavior, running from first base directly to second. After several successful trips around the diamond, we were ready for the next game. On game day, I was taking no chances—we bought more M&Ms.

We told Matt he could have the candy after the game if he could run the bases. The next time Matt was up to bat, he hit the ball and ran to first. Safe! On the next hit, Matt ran to second. Safe again! On the next hit, Matt ran to third. Safe? Oh no, he's out! Go back to the bench. Oops.

Nothing could keep him from his mission to complete the run. No one could make him leave the field until he touched that plate. Game play was halted as we tried to get Matt off the field. We had taught him to go in order: 1, 2, 3, and home. He couldn't bear anyone trying to interrupt the sequence. No, no, no. His protest was obvious to all as he lay down on the ground and wouldn't move. By that time, my husband, Tom, had gotten down to the field. He picked him up and carried him off the field toward me, my hands open to reveal the precious M&Ms.

So we needed to work on this game a little. Over time Matt figured out that even if he didn't make it home, we would still be near the bench with M&Ms in hand awaiting his arrival. His smile upon seeing his M&Ms was precious, so triumphant, regardless of the score.

M&Ms. Who would have thought that a simple bribe of candy could become a communication tool? We started using M&Ms as bribes for several teaching moments—because they worked! Don't worry, his teeth were fine, not a cavity until his twenty-second year.

There's more to the story, after all, there's more to T-ball than just hitting the ball and running the bases (we should know!). There's the outfield. Could he catch? Could he chase a ball? Yes and yes…well, kind of. He would go get the ball and throw it (not much power, but dead-on trajectory). Alas, his poor teammates could never figure out where or to whom he was throwing the ball because, as was his way, he looked sideways, out the corners of his eyes. Then again, no one else was a superstar either. It's one of the joys of T-ball. Ah yes, the comic relief of T-ball.

The children of T-ball are all young and just learning the game. A fly ball with a great chance of success to be caught could just as easily be dropped or left to fall where it may if a plane flew overhead. Every child in the outfield would jerk their head skyward to watch a gleaming plane write white-cloud lines against the blue of the sky. Even runners would stop and watch. A child in the outfield could just as easily not notice a ball because a beautiful butterfly just happened to be near, the fluttering of its wings much more exciting than a baseball rolling in the grass. So Matt's behaviors were taken in stride. He just didn't seem all that different from his neurotypical teammates when viewed in the light of T-ball.

The team went on to become champions, and each child received a shiny gold plastic trophy to commemorate the season. For Matt, it was a badge of honor—he had played T-ball. For us, it meant something too—*Matt had played T-ball!* He beat the odds. He chose to actually be around others, at a distance, but still close and still his decision. The second season brought another wonderful round of butterflies in the outfield and planes overhead and another great scorecard.

A writer from the local newspaper even came to watch the game, watch Matt play, and do an interview. I heard through the rumor mill later that a few parents claimed my son couldn't possibly be autistic because he played T-ball. Such was the thinking back then. But we didn't listen to those that claim "he couldn't" and listened instead to our own hearts and to Matt. All I knew was that anything was possible as long as I had a handful of M&Ms.

THE DEVIL COACHES SOCCER

NOT ALL SPORTS activities went well. Matt loved T-ball, and so did we. He loved the Special Olympics—at least until it dawned on him what the "special" meant. When he entered high school, we wanted his desire to play on teams to continue. "Team." Just the word oozes social skills, doesn't it? So we thought about each sport offered at the high school level.

Football—no. Matt was too nice to knock someone down, not very fast compared to other kids his age, and wouldn't know what to do if he ever got the opportunity to even touch the ball. He would be tackled and not know how to deal with it. No, certainly not football.

Baseball—unfortunately no. Although Matt loved the game, the level of sportsmanship was pretty terrible. Student jocks would resort to picking on him, and Matt couldn't deal with that type of situation.

Basketball—no, not after the fiasco of basketball at the elementary level (and that's another story altogether). The more we looked at each sport, the more we felt it would not be in Matt's best interests. That was until we looked at soccer.

Soccer consisted of both boys and girls. There would be running and kicking, and the directions for play were easy to understand. It was a new sport to the high school, and kids from all five grades could play (eighth to twelfth grades). Matt was in eighth grade, and Christopher was in twelfth. Christopher could watch over him and keep the bullies away. It felt right. We met with the coach and explained Matt's needs. We asked him, more than once, if he would actually play Matt. If Matt was to be relegated to the bench, then we would rather not do it at all. The coach assured us Matt would play, and he assured us each time we asked. He explained that when a game is obviously one-sided and there was no possible way the other team could win, that he always put in the less-experienced team players so that they could get some game-time practice. Sounded okay to us.

We went soccer shopping. The boys needed soccer shoes and accessories, and we were only too happy to oblige. It would be the only time in their school years that both boys would be on the same team—we were hyped! We took them to practice and stayed on occasion to watch some of the practice sessions. There were a few instances where we could see from the bleachers that Christopher was upset—okay, more than upset, he appeared really steamed! Each time we inquired about the problem, he gave the same answer, "The coach doesn't let Matt practice much or play." We would soothe his ruffled feathers by telling him that we had the coach's word that Matt would get to play eventually. Christopher was not so sure.

After each angry burst from Christopher, we would find the coach and restate our concerns.

"Are you sure you will play Matt?"

"Oh, absolutely! Yadda, yadda, yadda."

You know where this is going, right?

Several games came and went, and Matt's feet never touched the turf. We were getting concerned. The game at GW high school verified our concerns. The boys ran out on the field with the team following their coach to the bench. Matt is visibly excited again, hopping and pacing—maybe this time he will play. Christopher was more stationary, watching each quarter unfold. It was a new sport, and the kids on our team were not yet seasoned. They were being run into the ground by their opponent, and the clock kept ticking. It was obvious by the last quarter that the other team had beaten them thoroughly, and yet only the best players were still playing. No one who had sat on the bench for the last hour had gotten a chance to play. Time was running out. Tom and I fumed. How could the coach be so cruel to all those other kids? We would rather Matt not play on the team than to be on the team and not play. I wonder what the other parents thought as they too watched their children sadly sitting on the bench. Matt had been returning home after each game depressed and withdrawn.

No more! Just as we are making our plans to pull him from the team, we see Christopher yell at the coach. We see the coach yell back. We see Christopher grab his jacket and yell to Matt to get his coat.

We hear the coach threaten Christopher, "Don't you walk away from me!" Christopher pretending not to hear.

"You walk off this field and you're out! You will never play!" the coach continued.

"We're not playing now, what difference would it make!" yelled Christopher as he helped Matt with his coat.

Christopher proceeded to take Matt off the field. We were anxiously awaiting them as they climbed the steps toward the bleachers and away from the field.

"What was all that about?" I inquired, already knowing but needing to hear it from him.

"That SOB was never going to play Matt, he was never going to play anyone except his favorites, and I wasn't going to just stand there and let him hurt him like that!"

Now maybe I'm not the greatest of parents, but I sure was proud of my oldest son that day. He told the coach exactly what he thought—no fear. He stood up for his brother. Right is right and wrong is wrong, and what that coach did was wrong.

Tom went in to talk to the principal the next day, still fuming from the previous night's game. He was going in to file a formal complaint and, in doing so, showed tremendous support for the actions of our oldest son, Christopher. All we wanted was for Matt to have a chance to play. Game after game, practice after practice, the coach left Matt on the bench. We had explicitly asked the coach if he would ever play Matt to avoid this exact situation. All the coach had to do was tell us straight, and none of this would have occurred. Personally, I'm kind of glad it did. I am still over-whelmed with emotion when I think of how Christopher stood up to an adult, risked detention and reprimand, to stand up for his little brother. I would have done exactly the same thing.

Matt was initially upset, but he took his cue from his big brother and decided to dislike the coach too, telling me that the coach "was the devil." We found other activities to involve Matt. We moved on. I won't ever forget it though. And Christopher, if you're reading this, I know I have told you before, but I am going to say it again—you made me so very proud of you that day. I love you, kiddo.

DENTAL BASICS

WE WERE GETTING ready to go to town. Matt had only been up and moving for about an hour.

"Did you brush your teeth?" I asked.

"Um, yes!" he replied as he headed down the hall.

"Did you put on deodorant?" I asked.

"Um." He turned on a dime and headed straight for his bathroom.

Sometimes Matt needs a little reminder when it comes to personal hygiene. A little reminder is nothing if you could have seen the early years. Teaching an autistic child to brush their teeth, comb their hair, take a shower, put on deodorant, and for males, shave, are all an adventure in persuasion techniques. But of all of these personal hygiene lessons, the one that was worrisome right from the start was taking care of his teeth.

Parents brush a child's teeth for them until they can take the reins and do it themselves. An autistic child has obstacles to overcome that other children do not. The taste, the feel of the bristles, the gag reflex. We were lucky in that the taste wasn't too bad. Matt started trying different candies including candy canes at Christmas, and that same mint flavor was in toothpaste. Compare that flavor to brands with baking soda and soon you realize that baking soda toothpaste was a waste of time and money.

As for bristles, we started with a very soft toothbrush and had him explore the feel on his teeth at his own speed—a slow, timid sweep across the teeth, then another, and another. The back teeth caused a gag reflex, and he had difficulty overcoming this, and until he did, those back teeth didn't get much cleaning. I worried myself sick thinking about all the cavities he would have because his teeth were not getting the proper brushing. I knew it was time to see a dentist.

The first dentist trip was a complete disaster. Matt was four years old and absolutely refused to sit in the chair. I had to hold him…tight. Once we were in the chair, he refused to open his mouth. The dentist never saw Matt's teeth that day. I needed to find a special children's dentist, a specialist with struggling, refusing kids that didn't open their mouths. I called for an appointment and almost in the same breath explained that Matt was autistic. At that time, most people had never heard of autism, and I simply followed my statement with a short explanation of what autism was (as usual). The weeks prior to the visit, we practiced opening his mouth on command.

"Can I see those pretty teeth?" I asked. After several minutes, he would smile, and I would tickle him. "Can I see those pretty back teeth?" I ventured a little further.

Matt would open his mouth to show me, and I tickled him again. The game was simple enough, but would it work at the dentist's office?

It sounds like a nice, smooth transition, but it took more perseverance than you think. It took weeks of practice just to get him to open his mouth and let me see. Sometimes tickling wasn't enough. Sometimes it took bribes of cookies and candy and toys. It required a great deal of patience. Matt's dental exam with a pediatric dentist lasted all of five minutes. The dentist got a quick look, but that was all.

I continued to worry about his teeth, and finally decided I would take Matt to my dentist. I took both my sons, Christopher and Matt. The first visit was my appointment. Matt met the dentist and explored the waiting room and watched as the dentist looked at my teeth. Then I made the boys' appointments to coincide with my next visit. Christopher and Matt were both a bit anxious come appointment day. So was I.

Matt, hands flapping, watched as Christopher headed right in when his name was called. If Christopher had flinched, even a little, then Matt would have fought us. Fortunately, Christopher did exactly what he was asked to do, showing no fear. Matt willingly came back with me and watched as they looked at my teeth. When it was Matt's turn, he climbed into the chair on his own. The chair hummed as it lifted. I caught his eyes and smiled and pointed at my teeth. Matt understood immediately and smiled. The dentist asked him to open up, and I caught his gaze again and opened my mouth real wide. Matt again understood and responded by opening his mouth real wide. The dentist lightly touched each tooth. We had practiced this at home. Matt expected it and thus allowed the examination to continue. Afterward, I took the boys to McDonald's.

Sounds a bit strange, taking them to eat after having the dentist clean their teeth, but a bribe is a bribe, and Matt had been promised a treat if he allowed the dentist to look. Besides, breaking routine at this crucial point would have been disastrous. The next big step was changing toothbrushes. Matt never did like using a manual toothbrush. His brushing technique needed changing, and I couldn't get him to brush thoroughly with a manual toothbrush. Then the automatic toothbrushes came on the market, and that changed how well Matt brushed. The battery-operated spin brush was a blessing. Matt didn't mind brushing his teeth if he could use the automatic spin brush. Matt finally began brushing the back teeth because the spin brush did not cause a gag reflex.

Matt didn't have a cavity until 2009, at the age of twenty-three. I dreaded the day he would need a cavity filled, but I didn't need to. By then, Matt was well known at the dentist's office, knew the routine, and liked his dentist. I explained what would happen and gave him every single detail of the procedure. I told him his face would feel a bit weird but that it would wear off.

On the day of the appointment, I was the one that was anxious. Matt went in when his name was called. I watched him march through the door determined. A few minutes later, my name was called, and I went in to have my own scheduled cleaning. I sat in the chair straining to hear anything that resembled a fearful cry, pain, anger…but no sound ever erupted. After my cleaning, the dentist walked in to check my teeth.

"Matt had two cavities filled, and he's all done," he said, matter-of-fact.

I sat stunned. Really? Already?

"He needs to focus on his gums more…" the dentist went on. But I didn't hear him finish. My mind was still on the fact that Matt allowed a needle in his mouth, allowed the sounds of drilling and the feel of packing a tooth with filling. I was awestruck. Could it really have gone that well?

I met Matt in the waiting room. He didn't look happy, but he didn't appear fearful or mad either. Actually, he looked fascinated by the numbness of his face, and that was all. I schedule one more appointment for him to get a third tooth filled. On our way to the car, I explained to Matt that we would have to come back in a few weeks to do it again. "Yes," he replied. There was no fear in his voice. He never even flinched.

Matt is now twenty-eight years old. He brushes his teeth and sees his dentist twice a year. It's just another routine now. There are some possible oral surgeries in his future as his wisdom teeth have erupted, and one of them is stuck partially emerged and pushing on another tooth. We have upgraded the toothbrush to a Sonic with a two-minute timer, and it has a gentle touch on those sensitive gums of his.

Seeing the dentist is always a bit stressful, but I bet it probably is for most people, not just those with autism. I am a bit worried about surgeries, but I have to take it one day at a time. For now, taking care of his teeth only requires a simple reminder: "Matt, did you brush your teeth?" If more is required, then more will be done, and I know after all these visits that Matt will handle it, whatever may come.

MEMORY LOSS...
ARE WE ALONE?

THERE'S SO MUCH variance in autism that sometimes it's difficult to connect with others having similar problems. Some autistic individuals have food allergies and gut problems, some have seizures, and some autistic people have more than one disorder piled onto their autism. The possible problems that can accompany autism seem infinite, and yet with all the variances on the spectrum, I have not come across any mention of memory loss. I have been searching for information on memory loss in autism for quite some time, but alas, I have been unsuccessful in my quest. It occurred to me that Matt may be alone in this aspect of his autism. Is he?

Many autistics have a great memory. Matt has always had a wonderful ability to retain scientific facts and thousands of snippets from history. He can learn how to do something very quickly by recalling directions almost word for word. He has had this gift as long as I can remember. Unfortunately, his memory for people, places, and events of his childhood are gone—completely gone. He has no memory of being a young child and cannot recall an instance of his life prior to the age of ten. Is this because Matt, my son, is moderate/severe on the autism spectrum? It's not easy finding others with the same degree of autism to ask. Most autistic people I come across on my search are those on the milder side. They are articulate, in both speech and in their writing. None have ever mentioned memory loss, not one. I assume that if I actually met someone more like Matt, someone very autistic, that they would have greater difficulty in their ability to converse or write or possibly even understand my question, but I would at least attempt to ask it. I know I could be wrong, but I may never get the chance as the more severe cases are still quite rare. If this is the case, that moderate to severe autistic individuals can suffer memory loss of their childhood, then I feel it's something I need to put out there if only to make more people aware that there is even a problem in this area.

It began when Matt was on the cusp of puberty. Many of his autistic behaviors had disappeared by then: hand flapping, spinning, echolalia, avoidance of eye contact, need for routines, and so on, had slipped away one by one. He still loved repetition in both drawing animated characters and in watching his favorite movies and cartoons, but I understood that this was his way of teaching himself conversational speech and social interaction. I never thought of it as detrimental (and I still don't). He was doing well in school and was on the honor roll every time. He needed time to himself each day, and I gave it to him. He seemed so happy and content. He was more aware of his peers and wanted to dress like them, walk like them, and was attempting more complex interactions with longtime friends. He even had a few sleepovers during that time with a friend coming to our house one night and then Matt spending the night over at his friend's house. Life was not perfect, but hope did shine brightly.

Then one day I heard sobs coming from his room and went to investigate. Matt was sitting on his bed crying. I sat next to him and put my arms around him and hugged him tight. "What's wrong, Matt?" I asked as I rocked him slowly side to side. "I can't remember," he replied. I assumed he felt sad but didn't know why. Sometimes hormones do that at puberty, and in my quick assumption that he was experiencing a prepubescent hormone surge, I didn't prod him for a deeper explanation. He continued to cry. The anguish surfacing in giant waves of despair were tearing at my soul. "I don't remember *anything!*" he screamed. It took me by surprise. Not anything? What does that mean? "What do you mean, Matt, that you can't remember anything?" And so the conversation began in which my son explained to me that he really could not remember being a child. He could remember last week, last month, and some of last year, but the further back we went, the more obvious it was that most of his childhood memories were gone, all gone.

This was not a one-time instance. Over the next few years, Matt had more days of sheer panic where he couldn't pull up in his memory even important events he wanted desperately to hold on to. When all was said and done, Matt had lost everything before the age of ten and 70– 80 percent of everything from age ten to graduation at age nineteen. We're talking years of memories slipping away, and although new memories were being formed every day, only a few were actually staying in his mind for recall. Calming him, comforting him, during this time was heartbreaking for me too. I couldn't imagine how awful it must feel to not know something about your past. I would bring up certain instances from his past, trying to jog his memory, but although my intentions were good, it only made him feel worse. Amazingly, Matt stayed on the honor roll the entire time he endured the destruction of his own personal life history. It seems his short-term memory was still intact, and as a result, grades remained stable.

The turmoil ended as adulthood set in and he again has memories of people, places, and events—but only of the last eight to ten years. I think about it—almost obsessively. There are a few possible culprits that could have caused this dramatic change in his memory. During that particular time, Matt had concurrently gone through puberty, had pneumonia (and had to be hospitalized for almost a week on IVs and antibiotics), and had a pneumovax shot shortly after his recovery. Since Matt is the only one who knows when it all began and he can't tell me, I am left to wonder. Was it one of those? Was it the combination of all three?

So I research the blogs and the autism sites trying to find a hint that other autistic children have experienced something similar only to find silence in this area. There's no mention of this terrible aspect of his autism in others that I am aware of, and yet, I can't help but feel someone else had watched this heart-wrenching scenario play out in their own child. In my soul I feel there are others. Are there? I have come to the conclusion that what I must do is just ask straight out—have you ever known anyone with autism to suffer childhood memory loss? As a parent or a grandparent of an autistic child, I know you understand why I need to know, why I have to ask. So I am asking you, from one parent to another, are we alone?

THE EASTER EGG HUNT

WHEN I WAS a child, Easter meant candy in baskets and Sunday school. I remember the baskets quite well—full of Easter treats and hidden in a secret place. Upon waking, my siblings and I would immediately go on the hunt. Each basket had a name and the rules were if you found someone else's basket, you were to leave it be, not say a word, and move on. When our children were small, I wanted them to have the same experience. Tom and I would buy four baskets, fill them with candy, and hide them around the house. After a few years, the kids got too good at the hunt and the baskets would be found almost immediately, which is absolutely no fun for the adults, so we started a new tradition, the Easter egg hunt.

I had always taken the kids to the Easter egg hunts at church or at the local outdoor mall event. The church eggs were hand-dyed colored eggs—real ones, hardboiled. Pretty, but not all that desired by our troop of chocoholics. Church was difficult as Matt was still very young and spent the sermon under the pew. When egg hunting time finally came, he was ready to go home as he couldn't stand all the noise and commotion of the hunt. The outlet mall lawn had eggs everywhere, but a big brightly costumed rabbit stalked him, and the other children snapped up eggs right in front of him—leaving him with maybe one or two in his basket and tears on his face. After experiencing the public egg hunts, we decided it was time to start having one at our own home, in our own yard, with plastic eggs containing small wrapped pieces of candy—an event exclusive to just our four kids.

Our first family egg hunt was a small affair with only forty brightly colored plastic eggs. Into each egg was placed a small candy treat, and then each was placed in a big bag, ready for night delivery to hidden locations around the yard. The night before the hunt, Tom and I would venture outside after the kids went to sleep. Equipped with flashlights and a bag of eggs, we ran around to hide them in every conceivable place around the yard—under the downspout, behind a tree, under a leaf, nestled in a patch of newly sprouting weeds. Only a few could be seen from the back door, just enough to get them excited. Next, we placed four chocolate bunnies on the kitchen table—three small and one large. The next morning the children were told that the one with the most eggs got the giant chocolate bunny. We thought a competitive nature would please them, and it did—all of them except for Matt. I accompanied Matt on the hunt, taking him by the hand and leading him to the eggs I had hidden in the most camouflaged of spots. Sometimes they were there, sometimes they weren't—we had three other children all gifted in candy search techniques, and it was hard to keep a fair number available for Matt to find. Upon finding an egg, Matt would bend at the waist, pick up the egg, and open it, dropping the candy into his basket.

"Matt, we need to open the eggs later, you need to keep searching," I would prod. No matter how much encouragement I gave, Matt could only go slowly and methodically. The end result was just a handful of eggs. That meant that he didn't win the giant bunny, and this upset him tremendously. The smaller bunny in his mind signified he had lost, and losing to him was like a slap in the face to his self-esteem. His tears just about killed us. We realized we had made a serious mistake in making the giant bunny prize a reward for the most eggs—Matt would need years to perfect a search method and increase his speed, and we were not willing to go through each year's event if tears of sadness were the end result. Upon realizing we were definitely not doing this right, we decided to come up with new rules.

The next Easter we came up with the Prize egg. All eggs were not created equal. One egg had the word "Prize" written in marker, and the child to find that particular egg would get the big bunny. Each of the other kids felt bad about the prior year's tears and Matt's broken heart. We talked to them when Matt was busy in his room and asked them for their permission to let Matt find the prize. All agreed—wholeheartedly. The next morning we again released the candy sleuths to a yard with even more eggs than the year before—sixty, I think. Each of the children—Christopher, Jacob, and Sarah—found the prize egg and would smile. Christopher kept pointing at it, "Matt, over here!" Jacob saw it and moved it so the egg could be seen better, "Hey, Matt, there might be eggs over here!" Sarah saw it. "Matt, did you search here yet?" Matt made his way toward all the smiling faces. He looked down and around for a bit as each child looked at each other and smiled. Finally Matt saw the egg. He picked it up and held it above his head like a trophy, his smile a mile wide. Matt won the prize bunny, and each of us rejoiced with him. The next year we changed it again, making four prize eggs, each the name a specific child on it so that only that child could pick it up and claim his or her big chocolate bunny. No hurt feelings, everybody won, and the competitive nature was retained for the three older kids who were dying to compete against each other. Each wanted the title of the "One who found their prize egg first." Matt didn't care about that title—he just wanted to claim his prize.

Our annual egg hunt grew each year—from forty eggs that first year to over two hundred eggs the last year. Each year was a new adventure. We had hunts in the rain, watched eggs float by in a flood, hid some so well we didn't find them for years (ew!). Unfortunately, as the kids got older, scheduling a hunt became a nightmare, and eventually the annual egg hunt faded into memory.

It seems we did a lot of that kind of thing while the kids were small—the making of our own family traditions and celebrations. Subjecting Matt to the social interactions of an uninformed public was always so stressful with unsolicited comments that hurt me and I know Matt could hear. His autism was never a big deal if we just did our own thing, in our own way, with just our small cohort of six. I know it was not just better for Matt; it was better for all of us. The kids interacted with each other and with Matt better if they didn't have the public looking down their noses at them. We were all less stressed, and because we had our own strong nucleus to surround Matt, we could shake off the stares and comments of those whose opinions didn't really matter when we were subjected to them. It made us all more resilient and more compassionate. Developing our own way of doing things, like a private Easter egg hunt in our own yard, allowed us to concentrate on the things in our small group that really did matter—smiles, interaction, empathy, trust, and love.

ADVENTURES IN SOLs

FIRST, LET ME say I hate standardized testing. It hasn't turned out to be the cure-all for education that people envisioned. In Virginia, the standardized tests are called SOLs—I kid you not. No, SOL does not mean what you think. It stands for Standards of Learning. Not one good teacher actually thinks they are helpful—mostly they are considered to be a cruel slap in the face to true learning. Students only learn how to take a standardized test, not think. They must be taught only what is on the test, and when they get to college, they lack study skills and desire to learn. Students feel the instructor should only present them with what's going to be on the exam. So in other words, students are taught to memorize certain facts that are then easily discarded as soon as the test is over. Learning to actually think has now become the sole job of higher education.

Having said my piece about the sad content of SOLs, I will now tell you about Matt's adventures in standardized testing. They start testing early on—in elementary school. Matt took each standardized test along with his classmates. They made him a wreck. He couldn't sleep and cried and begged not to go to school. Yet year after tortuous year, he took and passed each exam. Matt has a great memory for facts. SOLs do not require any real critical thinking skills, just the ability to memorize, and Matt could memorize just fine. Matt did well in each subject: math, history, science, reading. It was English that was his sore spot—of course it was! He's autistic.

MATT WITH HIS PARAPROFESSIONAL, PAT

Autism is a communication disorder. English is how we communicate. It was fully expected that he would have difficulty in written communication. Matt's writing skills improved each year, but let's face it, he wasn't a great writer. He never saw the need for the little words: "it," "is," "of," "at," "the," etc. Leaving out the little "useless" words always affected his grade. The only class Matt ever took in high school where he didn't make an A was English—he got a B. He could read, he could do his homework, and he could write, albeit not as perfect as we would like, but well enough to make a point and demonstrate knowledge.

To graduate with a regular diploma, Matt needed to pass all of his SOLs, including English. The English SOL has two parts: one covers the parts of speech, spelling, and grammar—which is multiple choice—and the other one covers actual writing skills. Students are given a writing prompt and instructed to write several paragraphs on the subject. Matt flew through the multiple choice with no problems. He made an excellent score on that half of the test. His writing, however, was not very good (those pesky little useless words!). The overall score is an average of the two tests together. A student needs a 400 to pass. Matt received a score of 378. This was in his junior year of high school. He could retake the test again in his senior year.

You can bet it was an intense meeting of the minds that spring as we came together for Matt's last IEP. Some were convinced he would not pass and started throwing around the idea of a certificate of attendance in lieu of a regular diploma—it didn't go over well with me. I immediately took that idea off the table. Matt had not worked that hard, received all those excellent grades, and repeatedly made the honor roll year after year, simply to end up with a lousy certificate. Once that was cleared up, we began to construct an IEP that focused heavily on Matt's writing skills.

Test time came all too soon in the fall of his senior year. His score for his second attempt was 398. Damn! He missed passing by two lousy points. This was really beginning to get under my skin. How could they prevent my son from walking across that graduation stage simply because his writing skills—his communication skills—are slightly diminished because of his disability? It's like saying that because he is autistic, he can't graduate. I called the ACLU.

The ACLU works to stop such injustices. They took up the case and began giving me ideas on how to get the SOL for writing waived. The Virginia SOLs have a backup for English. Students can submit a portfolio of their writing—from several years of classes—and be scored that way. Oops. Who kept writing samples for the last few years? Where was this rule when we were discussing Matt's performance at the IEP? A portfolio was a great idea, but we didn't have the required materials for the year. It was now spring and graduation was looming. Matt had one more opportunity to take and pass the writing portion, and the test date was almost upon us.

I was a wreck. The Virginia Department of Education was holding their breath, Matt's teachers were pushing him hard, and his aide was completely stressed out. The ACLU was waiting for the results—would we be going to court to fight this requirement on behalf of autistic children? Matt was also a wreck. He begged not to go to school. I told him this was the last time I would ever make him take this exam. I told him that I knew, his daddy knew, and his brothers and sister knew that he was intelligent and wonderful, and no test in the world would ever change how we felt. Matt grudgingly took the English SOL writing section for the last time.

We had to wait a month for the results. Graduation was just weeks away, and we were on pins and needles. Then the news came—both written in his notebook and by phone. Matt had gotten a score of exactly 400! Talk about a celebration! Oh my, what a relief. There may not have been dancing in the streets, but there sure was a lot of dancing (and jumping and high-fives) at our house! His teachers smiled again, his aide could breathe again, the ACLU closed the file, and I imagine the entire Virginia Department of Education probably went out to slam back a few to celebrate their good fortune.

The following weeks were filled with awards banquets, and Matt was honored at each. Academic letter, honor roll, top 10 percent (number four in his class with a GPA of 3.81), Who's Who Among High School Students, and the National Honor Society. It was one celebration after another.

Finally, the long-anticipated graduation day arrived, and on a hot spring morning, our family gathered together to witness the impossible. My son, my beautiful baby boy who I was told would never be able to do anything, whom I was instructed to place in an institution, marched into the packed gymnasium along with his classmates. He sat next to his best friend, and we could see them smiling and conversing. Then his entire row stood up and marched toward the stage. I held my breath as I watched, tears in my eyes, as my son, now a young man, walked toward the stage, head held high, honor cords around his neck, and stepped onto the stage where he shook hands with the principal as his name was read.

And there, for the entire world to witness, a hard-fought battle was won as an honest-to-God true and wonderful high school diploma was placed into his welcoming hands. Matt had just beaten all the odds for those with autism graduating high school as he was the first autistic student in our county (and possibly in our state) to graduate. The road for other autistic children to do the same had just been made. It might not have been a clearly paved road, but it was visible...and a new hope was born.

THE MOTHER'S DAY TRADITION

MOTHER'S DAY. I should confess that before I became a mother I thought it was a holiday founded on guilt trips, one that forces one to buy something to prove their love. What child—young or old—wants to be thought of as the one who forgot their mom on Mother's Day? The guilt worked so well they decided to add another guilt-ridden holiday, Father's Day.

I will also confess that when I finally became a parent, I fell immediately into the trap of wanting to be the center of attention on Mother's Day. I blame all those Hallmark commercials... Anyway, all of that changed after Matt's autism set in. I came back to reality. It's not the expensive gifts of roses or jewelry or fancy dinners that are important. It's the hugs, the smiles, and the time you get to spend with your kids. When you get right down to it, it's really the incredibly simple things that bring the tears of joy on Mother's Day.

When Matt was little, holidays were a confusing, stressful time. Social get-togethers were too loud and complex. As far as Matt was concerned, gifts were for getting, not giving. It took him a long time to figure out the complexities for all the various holidays. For the longest time, he just didn't understand the social aspects of celebrating a Mother's Day. It's not like it's a birthday, it's not a holiday to share gifts like Christmas, and it has no special historical significance like July Fourth or Memorial Day. It's a hard day to explain.

I wasn't the best one to explain it either (as I still subconsciously harbored the idea of it as a guilt holiday to spur consumerism, which conflicted with the desire to be viewed as special because I had given birth). Fortunately, my husband has never been confused about Mother's Day (thank goodness!). He loves any reason to celebrate. For Mother's Day, my husband Tom, and sometimes my oldest son, Christopher, would add Matt's name to a gift or card, "From the both of us," as a way to include Matt in those early years. They have always managed to make the day a special one for me. Matt, on the other hand, had no desire to participate in such an obscure holiday. He still needed to learn to both express his thoughts and blend into social situations—and anything that involved social interaction or communication took time...lots and lots of time. What I didn't realize was just how much it would affect me when he figured it all out. It all started with a simple drawing.

Each year Matt watched as his siblings gave me cards, flowers, or some other token, and each year he heard the phrase "Happy Mother's Day" repeatedly. One year, after the presenting of cards and well wishes, Matt retreated to his room. I assumed the noise and commotion had bothered him and he left to seek solitude and quiet as he had done for every holiday, but I had assumed wrong. Matt soon reappeared with a sheet of paper and a smile. "Happy Mother's Day!" he said excitedly as he handed me the paper. On it was a simple drawing of a heart—a bit lopsided. The heart was drawn and filled in hurriedly with a regular number 2 pencil and next to it were the words "To Mama from Matt." The paper was folded in half like a card, and I opened it to find a drawing of the Powerpuff Girls (his favorite cartoon at the time) on the left side and "Happy Mother's Day" written on the right side. The cartoon drawing was expertly drawn and crafted. Time was put into the composition of the Powerpuff Girls. I was speechless. Matt had just presented me with his first card. He was eight years old, and it hit me like a ton of bricks.

Why did it hit me so hard? It was just a handmade card... Or was it? To create this card, Matt had to have put together social norms of the holiday (the card), a written expression of love (the heart), the correct phrase (Happy Mother's Day), and present-ing of a gift (the expertly drawn Powerpuff Girls). He had to have realized that the involvement in this celebration was impor-tant to me. To participate he had to overcome fear of noise and social interaction. Mostly, he had to overcome his fear of doing it wrong. I know many adult children that still fear a gift will not be "good enough" (when in reality the only thing the parent really wanted is to see them).

It was not just a handmade card. It was a testament to his courage and his desire to be included. I felt it deep within my soul. It reinforced the idea that autism was not static. Matt would continue to learn and grow as long as he could be brave and push himself past the fear. It was the understanding of how much courage and desire was required to present to me that card that brought the tears of joy on that Mother's Day.

That was the start of a new tradition. Every year on Mother's Day from that day to the present, I receive a drawing from Matt. This year will make drawing number 20. I have them all put away and look at each of them from time to time. Each year the picture is different, but the words are basically the same. He adds, "Love, Matt" and the date, but that is all. Each year I await the surprise. What will he draw me this year? Sometimes it's a picture of his favorite thing for that particular year. Sometimes it's something he knows I like. Sometimes he wants me to give him a suggestion of what to draw, whereas other years he remains secretive right up to the unveiling. At no other time of the year am I so excited by the receiving of a gift. It's such a simple thing—and yet so very powerful. I can't help but be deeply moved by each one.

His simple gift signified such an awakening. I know he had watched and learned quietly for many years before he connected the dots. I know that when he did make the connection, it took courage and a deep longing to fit in. He drew me a simple lop-sided heart and wrote a simple phrase, neither of which was all that "simple" for him. With autism, even the simple things require great focus, deep thought, and courage.

As a parent of an autistic child, you know how hard it is for your son or daughter to start something new, learn a social inter-action, or communicate an emotion effectively. And you know how hard it is to wait for the day when all that watching and learning from the sidelines begins to show. I can only say that it will begin—someday soon, I hope—and when it does, you won't be prepared for the enormity of it all. If you are like me, it will hit you like a ton of bricks. It will be one of the most intense and wonderful of feelings...and well worth the wait.

OUCH! NOT ANOTHER LEGO!

IT'S MIDNIGHT. THE house is quiet, children are sleeping, pets are sprawled out and snoring, and the house is dark and tranquil. "Ouch!" followed by a fury of words I won't repeat snaps through the still air. Another Lego block has cunningly found my bare foot. Why do I keep buying these things? After the hopping stops and rubbing my foot, I remind myself that these little booby traps are, well…needed. I tell myself to suck it up, put the block in the bucket, and just let it go.

Legos—the bane of parents everywhere and one of the most loved toys of children. We started with the big blocks (were they softer on the feet?), but soon went for the smaller version. Every one of our children loved to build. They built the item on the cover then, a few days later, would tear it down and design their own contraptions. My best friend, Carol, had already raised her boys and had a massive bucket of Lego blocks to donate to my kids (how many did she step on?). We had thousands, and many more were bought almost routinely. Christopher was the first to enjoy these sneaky little blocks. They exposed his creative side, his need to build, and even improved his reading skills. The directions for building are always in both written and diagram form,

allowing a child to work through the schematics and be triumphant in completion.

It was only normal for Matt to fall in love with them too. It
started simply enough: Matt lining up his cars, glancing toward
his brother out of the corners of his eyes, observing Christopher
sifting through blocks to create castles. Christopher would occasionally ask him to hand him a specific Lego. Confused at first as
to what his brother wanted, Christopher would describe it again,
and eventually crawl toward the block he wanted and pluck it
from the pile. Matt learned by observation and finally understood
the repeated requests. He would watch his brother snap and place,
decide on a block, snap and place. It was methodical and creative,
the finished product a recognizable masterpiece of the childhood
imagination. Soon after, Matt picked up a Lego and gave it to his
brother. This was soon followed by Matt attempting the snap-
together process himself. Before long, both were immersed in the
joy of Lego blocks. The building had begun.

In the beginning, Matt built trains (of course). He would dig
and dig through the bucket for each piece. No instructions, no
diagrams needed. Experimentation and observation allowed him
to see how something was constructed in his mind. The pictures
in his head must have become very complex, as it was during this
time that his drawings took on a complexity and detail not seen
in children his age.

The search for the right piece always followed the same
sequence of events: (1) plucking the first block from the bucket,
(2) digging, (3) dumping, (4) the hand-off, (5) completion.

PLUCKING THE FIRST BLOCK FROM THE BUCKET

Most of the time the first block was found quite readily. Usually,
the architectural design required a base plate and these were
fairly large and easy to find. It was the next few blocks that always
seemed to be elusive, and thus the digging.

DIGGING

The more blocks placed, the harder it seemed to find the next one, and the digging in earnest began. The sound of displacing Lego blocks is easily recognizable—a high "chink-chink" sound that could be heard throughout the house. Depending on the size of the project, the "chink-chink" could last up to an hour. Frustration and determination could only be borne so long before a new sound emanated from their room—the inevitable dumping of the bucket.

DUMPING

The new sound was like the crashing of glass on the floor, but not as high pitched. Once the bucket was dumped, the Lego blocks were spread across the floor in a semi-thin easier-to-hunt-through layer. We're talking thousands of blocks here. The spreading across the floor literally covered every available bit of floor space, trapping each child in their own small area, and thus, the need for the hand-off.

THE HAND-OFF

The teamwork and communication exchange was my favorite part. Christopher would ask for a piece. Matt would hand it to him. Scanning the floor, he would ask for another piece, but Matt would inevitably need that specific piece too and would reach it first and place it on his own masterpiece. This would cause a "Hey, I wanted that one!" from Christopher, and a laugh would erupt from Matt. Another race to a piece, "Ha! Got it!" from Christopher and another laugh from Matt. Christopher intuitively knew how to make Matt laugh each time. His comments were always in a fun voice, never harsh or condemning.

In the later years, when Matt was capable of words, the exchange would go both directions. Matt would grab up a piece and shout, "Ha!" and Christopher would feign disgust, "AGGGHH!" When Christopher retrieved that long-sought-after piece first, Matt would feign disgust, and Christopher would giggle to himself. It was an intricately choreographed dance of wits.

Building design evolved rapidly. As I stated before, the first projects were simple trains, but that didn't last long. More elaborate trains soon appeared. Hours upon hours of Lego building. Both boys could sit in the same room, hunting for pieces, interspersed with the occasional request (and sometimes denial) for far-flung pieces. They appeared to move together like a well-oiled machine, handing off blocks, sifting, handing off blocks. It was really quite amazing, this comfortable bond between them. Eventually, as skills improved, the desire to make new and larger objects (planes, ships, towers, castles) grew. Every Christmas and birthday brought a request for more Lego kits.

The bucket slowly filled to a heaping, rounded mound. This was no ordinary bucket. This bucket was a king-size rope-handled monstrosity that could hold two small children if needed. Get the idea? Thousands of Lego blocks, absolutely thousands.

New kits became available for trains, but most of the time the price tag was beyond our financial capabilities. Matt would have to use the pictures on the pamphlets to make the objects from the blocks he had. Small kits were purchased, which came with instructions that intensified his desire to do it exactly right. The need to be perfect was absolutely intense. He studied, he tried, occasionally failed (but only when he was a newbie), tried again. Eventually, Matt became the *Lego Master* (not to take away from Christopher's title of *Lego Ninja*). Jacob and Sarah would play on occasion, but they were not addicted and could turn their attention to other games and activities. Christopher could put them down to do something else for only a short time. He needed to return to complete the job eventually. Matt couldn't walk away.

When a task began, he had to see it to completion, and his hands whirled and twisted and darted out and back, picking up blocks and placing them just right. He could open a new kit of moderate size, pour out the blocks, open the instructions, and complete the kit in five minutes. *Five minutes!* On the rare occasion when we could afford the extravagance of a large kit, it would take him maybe six minutes. Returning from shopping, Matt would hurriedly walk to his room and emerge with the completed project triumphant in his hands before I was finished putting groceries away.

Happy and proud of his accomplishment, he would then hide the completed train, ship, plane, or car in a dresser drawer he reserved for such treasures. The drawer filled up and another drawer was readied (by tossing all his clothes on the floor). He hid them from the Lego Ninja. Obviously he wanted to make sure they would not be taken apart and used for other projects. Many of Matt's constructions used Legos from breaking down Lego Ninja's collection (and yes, of course it pissed him off, but he dealt with it, and for that, we were truly grateful!).

Ah yes, Lego blocks. Simple little blocks that taught interaction, manual dexterity, reading skills, and the deciphering of schematics. It enhanced creative play and required rigorous precision. It provided the venue for the bonding of brothers. Lego blocks initiated the slow demise for the lining up of toys. It helped to minimize hand flapping, allowing it to commence only during the scanning of the Legos spread across the floor. Matt's hands became much too busy plucking, snapping, sifting, and digging to flap. I watched Matt mimic normal behavior and got a glimpse of his desire to emerge from beneath his autistic exterior.

The years have gone by and Lego blocks have been stored away. Rooms have been remodeled, even new floors put down. Yet in the middle of the night, about a year ago or so, I walked quietly down the hall in my bare feet and...you guessed it, stepped on a Lego. One of the cats probably found it in the recesses of some dark corner and batted it into the hallway (or had it been hiding away biding its time until I least expected it and set a trap?).

Either way, when I think of Lego blocks, I think of the look of intense concentration, the whir of hands, the sounds of laughter, and the smile of a child triumphant. Legos, are they painful to the unsuspecting foot? Yes! Still…you gotta love 'em!

GPS? NO THANKS, I HAVE MATT

GPS (GLOBAL POSITIONING system), for all those with a crappy sense of direction, is now common in vehicles and phones. I don't need GPS. I have Matt.

I didn't know of his gift until after he began speaking, but the ability was present long before that. Matt was just four years old when we took our first trip to see relatives near Chicago, driving from our house in the mountains of southwest Virginia. Matt was not speaking yet on this first trip. He rode quietly in the backseat, staring out the window. Our other three children talked and laughed excitedly for hours until the sun went down then promptly conked out. Not Matt. He would fight sleep—just had to see where we were going—and continued to stare out the window. We drove most of the way at night because, well, we had four kids. The trip home was similar, and when the sun went down, all eyes closed, except for Matt's.

We didn't take trips up north very often. It cost money, and we live from paycheck to paycheck. So the next time we went up north for a visit, it was years later. Matt was speaking in simple sentences by then and with the coming of speech came the beginning of a new behavior, the outer monologue. I don't know if other autistic children do that, talk to themselves out loud, but Matt did. Speaking in a low voice, he would say what was on his mind. Maybe it helps him to focus on what he is doing. There are times when I talk to myself out loud, and usually it is when I am trying to stay focused on something I am doing, or working through a problem I am having. Have you ever talked to yourself out loud? In any case, it was a Godsend. His outer monologue gave me insights into his thoughts and allowed me to catch up on what scared him, bothered him, or even what he loved. When Matt spoke, I listened.

Matt spoke softly to himself while we drove the route from our house to my mother's, nine hundred miles away, and I wasn't able to catch what he was saying until the other children fell asleep and the car became quiet. I leaned back, straining to hear his voice and decipher the words. After a few minutes, I understood what he was doing—naming the roads, the signs, and giving the step-by-step, turn-by-turn direction for driving our route to my mother's home in Rockford. He had actually memorized the way to Grandma's house!

This was very enlightening in several ways:

First, wow! What a memory. He was accurate about every highway, off ramp, major road sign, even where we stopped for gas and bathroom breaks! He knew major interstates and every city street to take to reach our destination. The pronunciations were not always accurate, but the sequence was dead-on.

Second, a "lightbulb" moment, I realized that in order for him to do this, he had to have memorized the directions from our last trip, years before, when he was unable to communicate verbally. Of course, it makes so much sense now—roads form long, unbroken lines, connecting one major area to another, just like telephone lines, just like railroad tracks—all of special interest to Matt. His interest must have been intense as he never slept while the car was moving. He was too busy waiting for the next sign, the next turn, the next gas station.

Third, this was one of those moments that changed how I taught him. I realized that he was learning by watching and listening, and regardless of how many words he could say, he was learning, day after day, hour after hour. I had assumed that he learned through practice, practice, practice. Now I knew the truth. Everything was educational. Just simply being around the exchange of knowledge, such as in a classroom, or within earshot of a conversation, was providing him with the information he needed to make some great neural connections. I could teach Matt new things just by speaking out loud to myself within hearing distance, knowing he would not only hear what I said, but think about what I said. It was the gift of a new tool in the teaching-autism toolbox.

He retained this behavior throughout his childhood and into adulthood. What a wonderful gift it has been to me. And to this day, he memorizes directions and maps. When we go on a vacation to a destination he has never before been to, he still stares out the window, taking it all in. Sometimes he draws some of the road signs, and sometimes he draws a few landmarks (like statues or monuments). Rest assured, when we travel back to that same vacation spot even years later, he will give the step-by-step directions under his breath. He remembers every turn. If I ask him "Where do we turn next?" he sits up straighter, gets his bearings (this takes only seconds), and gives me the route to take, taking great pride in his ability to do so.

My sense of direction is pretty good, so I don't *need* to ask him very often, but I do. It initiates a conversation, gets him to speak to me on something he knows about, and he's always happy to help. Matt is always eager to provide technical assistance for any journey, whether a long trip or short. It's a part of himself that he likes, even if it was the autism that brought his GPS gift to the surface.

GPS? Not in my car. Why would I ever need GPS when I can have something much better, a conversation with my son?

WITH AUTISM, THERE'S NO SUCH THING AS A SIMPLE SHAVE AND HAIRCUT

I TRIED TAKING my autistic son, Matt, for professional hair care when he was little, but I soon found out the hard way that there was no such thing as a simple haircut. Matt, not wanting to sit in the chair, put on the apron, or watch a pointed object approach his head, would struggle and fight through the entire process. The struggle was so intense that he wore out the hairstylist, me, and himself. I finally decided that if he were to ever have a haircut, I would have to attempt to do it myself. I hoped that maybe being in the comfort of familiar surroundings of home, maybe, just maybe, we could be successful.

I talked him into sitting in the chair and even in wearing the plastic drape, but all that cooperation disappeared when I got out the scissors. As I tried to trim his hair, Matt would unexpectedly jut his fingers up between the blades of the shears in an attempt to stop the process. He squirmed, twisted, his hands in constant motion the entire time. He especially hated the sound of his hair being trimmed around his ears, his hands again flying upward to cover and protect them. It was exhausting for both of us.

Unfortunately, this would be our routine for quite sometime. With no professional to cut his hair and me as his hair stylist, the poor guy endured the trauma of a "simple" haircut time after time. I was pretty awful at it in the beginning and must confess there were several times the end result was absolutely ghastly. The only thought that allowed me to keep my sanity and lessen the guilt of the jagged edges and roller-coaster bangs was the knowledge that it would soon grow out again, a double-edged sword as the process of cutting his hair was also rife with guilt and stress.

So it turned out that a "simple" haircut was not so simple. The worst one was when he was three to four years old. The haircut was taking a very long time as I maneuvered around those tiny exposed fingers, trying to calm him with my voice while I brushed his hands away with one hand and cut his hair with the other. Having gotten just enough out of eyes and from around his ears and exhausted from the battle, I finally removed the drape, and he hopped down. Unfortunately, just when I was about to have that sigh of relief and thank my lucky stars for having not injured him, I witnessed one of the most heart-wrenching scenes. Matt stared sadly at his hair on the floor. With tears in his eyes, he bent over and slowly picked up a handful of scattered clippings and tried to place them back on his head. No matter how hard he tried, the hair simply slid off and fell back to the floor.

Each attempt was met with even more tears. Matt sat on the floor, mourning a piece of himself (his hair), a piece that was now lost forever. His gut-wrenching sobs forced me to see the experience from his eyes, and what I saw was terribly disturbing. I imagined he must have asked himself why. Why would his mother do this to him? Why would his mother literally remove parts of him and sweep it into the trash? I can't imagine his confusion or depth of despair at the forced removal of pieces of his own body, and as I thought about what he was going through,

I became racked with guilt. It made me realize that there is so much more to a haircut than simply cutting hair.

Matt didn't understand the why, and in his panic to save himself, he would risk bodily harm. I can, to this day, close my eyes and remember those tiny fingers trying desperately to stop me by getting between the strands of hair and the blade of the shears.

That was over twenty years ago. Some memories are difficult to erase. Realizing that my son actually thought I was trying to take a piece of him and throw it away shook me to my core. I learned an important lesson that day—everything, no matter how trivial it may seem, needed a why.

I am happy to say it got better after that. Having witnessed his despair, I came to realize that I had approached it all wrong. I should have cut his brother's hair in front of Matt, and probably his daddy's hair too. I should have let him feel the scissors and have him cut a piece of hair himself. I should have talked him through step by step and repeatedly for several days prior to the actual cutting. I understand now that Matt struggled and fought me because he was afraid. He distrusted me afterward because I had removed a part of him with no explanation as to why. I deserved it, for I treated him like a child.

In order for a simple haircut to be a simple haircut, I needed to take each step apart and explain the whys and show him examples of others having it done. He needed to see that it was okay, that no pain was involved. A simple haircut may have actually been a simple haircut if I had thought it out better. After a few years of practice and patience and the cooperation of both my oldest son and husband as role models, Matt's fear disappeared. He now comes willingly to the chair, keeps his hands under wraps, and checks the final style in the mirror to make sure it is to his expectations—all very normal behaviors. This could've happened sooner had I just known of his fears.

Matt didn't have his first professional haircut until he was twenty-seven years old. I had put it on his list of things to accomplish before he could live on his own so he could see it was an important step that had to be taken. I made an appointment for Matt with my hairstylist, Karen, who said she was honored to have been asked to give it a try. A few days before the appointment, Matt decided to cut his own hair, forcing me to reschedule. His attempt at a haircut was ghastly—almost as ghastly as those first few I had done. I had to talk with him and ask him not cut his own hair. "Please let Karen do it."

The big day arrived, and we used the occasion as a mile marker, complete with pictures and a nice dinner out afterward. Matt, knowing I was recording the event, smiled through his panic every step of the way.

Karen first asked him if he wanted his hair washed, and Matt referred to me with his eyes. I nodded. He replied yes. But his voice was more like "uh-oh." Then he went calmly (at least on the outside) to the chair at the sink. Karen was patient, spoke to him often, used lukewarm water, and massaged his head with shampoo slowly. Matt was impressed with how wonderful it felt and even managed a smile.

Next, she trimmed his hair, asking him his opinion and keeping him focused on the chore at hand and off the pointed object in her hand.

Lastly, she trimmed his beard. Matt looked in the mirror at me constantly for reassurance, and I smiled and kept telling him he was doing great, which he was. When it was all over, Matt used a hand mirror to reflect all angles off the larger mirror and proclaimed it was all good.

Wow! What a difference a professional cut made on his appearance! He looked great. Matt knew it too. Not only did he look like a million bucks, he also felt like it. Confidence radiated from him the rest of the afternoon. The hurdle of the haircut had finally been cleared.

Haircuts weren't the only hair problem we faced. Puberty brought many challenges with it and seemed to have arrived much quicker than anticipated. I was unprepared for the changes in his body, his voice, and his behaviors. Matt had learned to put on deodorant, brush his teeth himself, and now it was time for him to take his own shower without help or supervision. Prior to the onset of puberty, I had always run the water for him, brought in his clothes, got his towel ready, and midway through the splashing of toys would wash his hair. Then one day I noticed he had a small patch of pubic hair—it was time for Mom to back out and turn over the nightly bath to my husband.

The change in routine was difficult at first, but Matt was also becoming very aware of what other guys did, mainly his brother and Daddy, and was easily convinced to attempt the shower in lieu of a bath. In the beginning there were many failed attempts, times when all he did was get wet. He would emerge from the bathroom with a dirt ring still around his neck, his hair wet, but still greasy and dirty. I would have to send him back in to do it again. When I sent him in, I would give more detailed instructions, something he really needed. He learned quickly that I would inspect his neck and ankles and fingernails and smell his hair afterward, and this helped him to realize what was needed. Still, there were times in which I suspected he only washed those specific areas.

Next, Matt's facial hair had started to come in. We attempted the shave. I tried to help him once or twice, but let's face it, I don't shave my face and am not the right person to instruct him. I tried, really tried, but I just couldn't seem to help him do it right. My husband stepped in at this point and went over the procedure step by step, taking his time and explaining each part.

Matt had watched Tom and Christopher shave, and this helped to at least give him the courage to try it, for which I am thankful. Matt even thought the foam shaving cream was pretty cool and liked putting it on his face, but the fun stopped there. He hated the scratchy feel of a razor. His face always appeared irritated afterward, and soon acne started to form. After a few months of struggling with regular razors, we switched him to an electric razor—heck, what did we have to lose? Unfortunately, he hated the buzzing sound and the tug of the blades on his whiskers. He just couldn't stand it.

I understood. Matt was tired of having to rub this metal torture device across his face. Why? Not "why was it a torture device?" I got that. I meant, "why does he need to shave?" It seemed reasonable that there was still a choice left—keep the beard.

Matt was only in ninth grade when he begun to really grow out his beard. Christopher also grew out his facial hair, and Tom allowed his own beard to emerge again. The transition was drastic as Matt's face transformed to one with a beard. He looked so much older. To be truthful, he looked a bit scary—a big guy, a beard, and now a deeper voice too. What a huge transformation from my sweet little boy into the physically adult (and scary-looking) Matt.

He appeared so rough to my eyes that my first thought (and I kid you not) was, *This is definitely not someone you would want to run into in a dark alley.* I needed time to adjust.

Slowly, I was able to adjust. I actually began to like this new persona for exactly that reason. No stranger would ever think of him as helpless. This brought me some peace of mind, and I really began to enjoy this new look. Badass Matt!

So Matt takes showers, gets his hair trimmed on a regular basis, and has a beard—a really cool one. He lets Karen trim it up and allows her to thin it out to make it appear neat and tidy, but not because he needs it to look a certain way. I'm the one who wants it trimmed. He would let his beard grow to his feet if I let him (at the rate it grows, it could be that long in about six months). What I like is that Matt's happy with the way he looks. And although it took some getting used to, I am happy too. I have found that just as with most matters concerning my son, time and patience brings revelation and clarity. And although there was no such thing as a simple haircut for my young autistic son, success did eventually arrive.

He really has come a very long way, and through it all, I learned a lot about my son, about myself, and about autism.

THE ANGEL ON HIS SHOULDERS

THERE ARE TIMES when I think Matt walks with an angel on his shoulders. This week, my husband was offered a new position that would require him to work every Friday through Sunday and in exchange would pay him a great deal more. Our first response was "When would we see each other?" That was replaced soon after with the thought, *Oh my, Matt would have a backup for every single day*. You guessed it. We decided he should take it. It took about five minutes to decide.

That got me to thinking and reflecting back over the years and made me realize that this is no coincidence. Every step we take, every move we make, Matt has always been the blessed receiver of each new circumstance. Over the years, Matt was met with kindness, compassion, and new experiences. Each offshoot of our struggles and financial upheavals had always worked out well for him. He seems to naturally attract people that show him a bit of kindness, a bit of help, always just the right people at just the right time. In our tumultuous and chaotic life, we have been able to look back and see how even the loss of jobs sparked new developments that fit perfectly with what Matt needed at the time. Let me give a few examples.

There was the perfect interaction between Matt's teachers and myself over the years, from preschool to high school. I found teachers that would listen to my concerns and, although they were skeptical, allowed for the possibility that there was more to Matt than meets the eye. My grandma always told me you can get more with honey than with vinegar, and I rarely raised my voice and never started an interaction with anger. As a result, confrontations were few, acceptance and a willingness to go beyond the normal procedures were more apt to happen, and Matt felt the benefit every step of the way. That's not to say I didn't have my moments. I pushed when needed, even got angry a few times in order to relate what I felt needed to be done, but they were few and far between. The teachers knew I would never give up, and instead of fighting or arguing, they learned and put into practice the methods that gave my son a fighting chance.

But nothing was just given to him—ever. I never wanted that, and they knew it. I needed to know what Matt could really do and what he couldn't do, so there was no easy pass, and they respected me for that. They knew I wanted Matt to learn, not to be babied or get a grade for a grade's sake. He was intelligent in many ways, and once they saw that autism does not mean low IQ, they went for the creative instruction. Teachers from the previous year would help the teacher of the next year. I admire them for their concern and for upholding their educational standards. Matt's education was also blessed with two very wonderful aides that bonded to my son as if he were their own child. They always had his back—Matt's surrogates while at school. Don't get me wrong, it wasn't always a walk in the park, but it was made so much easier by the people that came into my son's life year after year.

Even his bus driver was a blessing. His bus driver, Mr. Jackson, drove Matt's special education bus throughout his entire school career. Mr. J was a gruff elderly fellow who saw something in my young son that immediately attached him heart and soul. He was always on the lookout for signs of distress, and never allowed anyone to come between Matt's bus ride routine and his destination. If Matt cried about anything, there would be hell to pay. When retirement came, he decided to put it off one more year in order to drive the bus for Matt in his last year. Such was the bond between Matt and Mr. Jackson.

There was an exceptional big brother who taught Matt games and interactions and became Matt's focus as to how to act, what to say, and most amazingly became the anti-bullying bodyguard. My oldest son, who as a senior had his handicapped little brother enter the same small school, did not see his little brother as an embarrassment. Instead, there was a fierce bond and a protection factor that prevented bullying, showing no fear to anyone. Misconduct by another person, regardless of whether they were student or faculty, were met with the wrath of the outspoken and fearless older brother, always putting his brother's feelings and safety first. My fears of bullying slipped away as his older brother had influenced an entire school. Even after he graduated, Matt had buddies and teachers who took the place of my older son, who stepped up and took an interest in his safety, in his feelings, and especially in Matt as a person, not just someone with moderate/severe autism.

As for me, my job took me from a career in the medical field to one in teaching where my schedule actually fell in sync with my son's. Teaching allowed me to spread awareness to a new generation, a generation who would know another individual with autism at some point in their lives, possibly in their own child. As my schedule became steady, my time to teach Matt increased. The bold strides he made, the accelerated progress of those years, were a culmination of so many new experiences and chances to teach him new things because I had the perfect schedule and more opportunities to meet his needs.

Even these past six years with alternating periods of joblessness and contracts for my husband has allowed his search for full-time work to provide a way for Matt to experience new places. Going with my husband took Matt away from home for weeks on end, practicing for life on his own. It also provided time for Tom to get to understand and communicate better with Matt and to become exceptionally close. And now, as Matt prepares to move, my husband's new work schedule will be the complete opposite of mine. What that means to us is that Matt will have one of us there for him no matter which day, no matter which hour. We will be there to support him when he needs us to help him and encourage him to go beyond what anyone else had ever dreamed possible but many came to dream with him just the same.

Yes, I think Matt has had an angel on his shoulders for a very long time.

Long ago when he was only five years old, I was watching him get out of his bus seat, grab his pack, and head for the door when he turned his head, said something, and gave a short wave behind him. There was no one on the bus except the driver, and he was up front in the opposite direction. As I held my son's hand and walked him back to the house, I asked him who he had waved to. He said only one word. "Angel."

Matt may not see that angel anymore, he may not wave or speak to him, but that angel is still there—watching out for my son, turning our lives upside down, sometimes for years on end— to make Matt's life the best it could possibly be. My prayer for my son, from his diagnosis to the present, have always been to give my son the chance to be who he needs to be. That prayer had been slowly answered in a thousand little ways over the past twenty-eight years. The steps were so small, so seemingly chaotic that it never occurred to me then. I never saw it back then. But I know now. God sent an angel.

LEARNING BIOLOGY USING EIGHT-LEGGED FREAKS

NOT EVERY PARENT can say they exposed their children to a room full of spiders...maybe I should clarify that.

I returned to college after I was laid off from my lab job in 1995 (when Matt was only nine years old) and decided to would work toward my bachelor degree in biology at Radford University. During my second year, I decided I wanted to do research. I had always loved science, especially biology, and had always wanted to do scientific research. I got my chance to learn the trade as a student under the guiding wings of Dr. Fred, a research biologist. His area of research was spiders—yep, spiders.

I chose to research how the male of a desert funnel-web spider (*Agelenopsis aperta*) knocked out the female prior to mating. My hypothesis was a pheromone, a chemical messenger that traveled through the air. Research takes hours upon hours of observation, and year after year of testing. I was also raising four children, and there were several times when my research time overlapped my family time. Consequently, in order to do both, I would take the kids with me on occasion, exposing them to a lab filled with spiders.

Sounds pretty scary, huh? It really wasn't so bad, after all each spider had its own little clear box, and a cover of course. There were approximately one hundred spiders in the lab, but they were contained, and the kids really wanted to see them, all except Matt. The first time I took them with me, Matt stayed in the hall, peering in on occasion to make sure we were alright. Jacob and Christopher spent most of their time trying to figure out the small sign posted on the wall that read, "Time flies like an arrow, fruit flies like a banana." Sarah was fascinated by the spiders themselves. I gave them a quick tour and showed them the video setup for taping the spiders' activities. Fred came by, and I introduced him to the family. He saw Matt in the hallway and stopped to speak to him. Matt was nervous and didn't say a word.

Each time we went by the lab, the kids got bolder. They took a closer look at the spiders and took another puzzled look at the sign. Matt came inside the door and looked around. If Fred was nearby, he would stop to say hello, and Matt, having recognized him from previous visits, began to greet Fred with a "hello" of his own. Matt became more comfortable with being in the lab and even got near enough to the containers of spiders to look inside. Most of our trips to Radford University included time to play on the campus. So although the reason for the trip to RU had something to do with the spider lab, it was just a small portion of the time we spent on the campus. Matt started to love these trips. He loved running with the other kids across the lawn and exploring the hallways of each floor of the science buildings. He especially loved seeing Fred, so much so that when I announced we were going to the campus, Matt would reply, "To see Freddy!"

I finally graduated from RU and finished my research a few years later. Matt was now in the seventh grade and needed to do a science project for the science fair. We talked about several things he could do, and he decided to do one about global warming (yes, it was occurring back then). He loved science—that is, except for biology. He never cared much for learning about the living organisms of our world and instead focused on the disastrous events of Mother Nature—earthquakes, tornados, landslides, icebergs. He chose to study how melting icebergs affect sea level. We worked on it together. I was the guide on how to set it up, and he was the tester and writer. He did very well on this project. This was important because years later he was required to do another science fair project for tenth grade for biology. He knew what he had to do, and although he absolutely hated homework and hated biology, he was not afraid of the actual assignment. We talked about this next project at some length. Nothing it seemed was of interest to him. Each idea I had was shot down, and Matt had no idea what he wanted to do.

I then had an inspirational idea—spiders! We had some very beautiful garden spiders making webs in our yuccas. Garden spiders are the bold black and yellow spiders that form a zig-zag pattern at the center of their web. I took Matt outside to see the spiders. I caught a grasshopper and tossed it on the web. Immediately the garden spider sprang into action, catching the insect and quickly wrapping her prize for a later meal. I was waiting for Matt's reaction. A sound of disgust would mean "No way!" A continued gaze would signal fascination. Matt did neither. Instead, Matt laughed.

Matt knew I hated grasshoppers. They had been destroying my flowers and vegetable garden, and I wanted to get rid of them. Unfortunately, I couldn't use insecticides for fear of harming one of our numerous pets. Matt also had seen the cult classic *Eight-legged Freaks* with me several times. The movie was far from scary and actually pretty funny, pitting people against spiders. Matt loved it.

I caught another grasshopper and handed it to Matt who quickly threw it on the web. Again he laughed at the lightning speed of the spider. Matt then caught a grasshopper on his own, the very first time he had actually touched a bug, and threw it on the next web. Again, the spider raced toward her prey, caught it and wrapped it, and again Matt laughed. His laughter convinced me we were on the right path.

Next we had to decide what to actually research. Matt decided to time the spiders to see how fast they could catch and spin. His hypothesis was that larger spiders could go faster than smaller spiders. Each afternoon we would head out to the yuccas. Matt took several photographs. He held a ruler up to each contestant and measured their length. We took turns in either catching the grasshoppers or timing the spider's race to catch and spin on a stopwatch. After collecting the data, I sat down with him to help him organize the material. I had to be so careful to not write this myself—it's a very difficult thing letting your child do all the work. Matt hated the writing part, his grammar was faulty, his spelling was weak, and his attention span was very short. But I sat with him each day and encouraged him to write one short paragraph at a time. Even one paragraph required several breaks, and this meant writing the paper and making the display board would take a lot of time. Matt just could not focus on it for more than twenty minutes at a stretch.

The weeks went by, and finally his project was complete. The title was "Spider Race," and he got an A and even went on to the county competition. It was a great experience for him. I was most impressed with my son during the judging of his display. Matt was asked a battery of questions by each of the judges, and he was able to give very detailed replies. His teachers, his aide, and of course, his family were all very proud of him. I still have the research paper and photographs he took.

Matt never would have done this sort of thing had he not been exposed to the spider lab at RU. His fear of bugs and spiders lessened over the years, and the biology no longer annoyed him. When he was young, I had to force him outside, but after his experiment in the garden with the beautiful black and yellow spiders, I never had to force him out the door again.

Matt has lost many of his memories over the years as he shed various autistic traits, but he still remembers the spider lab at Radford University and Fred. It must have had a great impact on him to have retained that particular memory. I guess you just never know what event will become a landmark in a child's life. No one would have guessed one of the landmark events in Matt's life to be one involving eight-legged freaks—the spiders.

DEALING WITH GRIEF

Grief can be an overwhelming emotion. It's a feeling of loss that pulls from both guilt and sadness. It sits deep within us wanting to get out, but we tend to block its path. We hold on to it, playing memory tapes over and over in our mind as we adjust to the change in our life. We understand what a person who is dealing with grief may be feeling because of our own experiences with it, but we should not assume we know how each person should express their grief. That is a misconception. Grief, with all its complexities, cannot be experienced in the same way by any two people. It's only logical then to assume that a person with autism will have their own way.

My son Matt, who is autistic, has had to deal with grief more than once in his short life of twenty-eight years. The first time he had to deal with death was as a young child around the age of nine to ten. He had a cat named Sweetpea whom he loved tremendously. We also had dogs at that time, but they were jumpy and loud, and Matt had little interaction with them. The cat was different. She approached him slowly, made her pleasure known in soft purring sounds, and was content to sit near him without annoying him. Unfortunately, having a pet, loving a pet, becoming attached to a pet also means you are willing to undergo the grief that will eventually come when the pet dies. We didn't think about that when we brought her home. We only thought of the smiles and laughter and the interaction Matt would have with a living thing.

Only a few years had gone by when the unthinkable occurred. Sweetpea was hit by a car. Not wanting Matt to endure the grief, we went ahead and buried the cat, and told him of her death afterward. We were definitely not prepared for his anger. Why did we put her in the ground? She can't breathe! She is afraid of the dark! He could not be reasoned with and could not be consoled. We did the only thing we could do—we dug her up.

After we removed her from her grave and unwrapped her body, we brought Matt out to say his good-byes. She looked as if she was sleeping, and he gently reached over to pet her. His hand quickly pulled away a split second after, realizing from the cold stiffness of her body that she was indeed dead. Matt and I talked about it over and over for days afterward. He had questions and sadness and guilt, and I did my best to answer him, comfort him, and take his guilt away. I learned a big lesson from that experience. Never hide the truth, even if you mean well.

Shortly after, we got him another kitten with similar markings, and he named her Sweetpea II. Sweetpea II is still going strong at twenty-plus years old and still his beloved cat. But someday... Well, we know what someday will bring.

Over the years I have noticed that Matt deals with an emotional situation very similarly as his older brother, Christopher. This really comes as no surprise to me as Matt has idolized his brother his entire life. If Christopher could do something, well then Matt could too. It was this desire to be like his older brother that spurred Matt into overcoming so many obstacles autism set before him. I like to think of them as my bookends of a full life: Matt is the light of my life and teaches me to see deeper, find the simple joys, and live happy every day, whereas Christopher is my pride and joy and holds within him a clear-cut view of right and wrong. He stands up for what he thinks is right with a tenacious determination and overwhelming presence. I am in continual awe of both my sons.

Emotionally, Christopher holds his grief deep inside. He guards his feelings. They are personal and not up for public review. He thinks deeply and feels deeply, but on the outside, he appears strong and steadfast. He will discuss with me his thoughts when, and only when, he is ready to discuss them, receive comments, listen to advice, or just needs a reaffirming hug. Christopher was only two years old when his brother Daniel died.

Daniel was born prematurely in 1984. I remember having to explain to Christopher why his little brother died. I told him he had been born too soon and his heart just couldn't take the strain. In his sadness, he never cried, but seemed to hug tighter, want to be next to me more often, and kissed the top of my head when I cried. He attended the funeral. He still didn't cry. I assumed he was too young to fully understand. Two years later as we were driving to his paternal grandparents' house, Christopher asked me a simple question, "How did Daniel die?" I again explained very simply that he was born too early and his heart just wasn't strong enough to keep going. He thought about that for a minute and then very sincerely suggested, "You can give Daniel my heart and then he wouldn't have to die."

His words hit hard. My son was willing to give his life for his brother to take away the sadness that I carried with me. How long had he thought about Daniel? How long had he been watching me deal with the grief? I didn't purposefully cry in front of him, but my despair was so deep that when I cried he knew why. He continued to understand even years later that I still carried that sadness deep inside, even if I no longer cried.

Christopher's same gift of empathy showed itself repeatedly over the years as Matt grew up. He taught Matt to interact, play games, tell a joke—the list is as long as his life. Christopher had given Matt his heart. In return, Matt looked to his brother on how to act—in the car, at a restaurant, at school, and around others. Christopher never thought about Matt's focus on him, not until I told him years and years ago. In retrospect, Christopher has always been Matt's guiding light.

Matt knows this instinctively about his brother. He holds himself to the same standards he has for Christopher. After all, if Chris can do it, then Matt can do it. Both take after me in the need to be alone when grieving. I do not wish to share my grief until I am ready, and that may be a while. We are different in that my initial grief is tearful, but then I put it deep in my heart and think it over for months, and in the case of Daniel, years, but tears are not for either of my boys. Neither wears their heart on their sleeve.

I realized this when we moved to Arizona. It was to be a temporary move as my husband had several contracts, and instead of surviving apart, we all went together: Matt, Tom, and me. Christopher was grown and was going to take care of our Virginia home during our absence. Matt seemed fine with the move, and all seemed to go well. We took each day as it came, trying to make every excursion an adventure. Matt never cried, never showed that he missed his cat, his home, or his brother—that is until we started discussing a more permanent move. Matt broke down, and all his fears came to the surface. He poured out his heart and told us he had been crying every night.

I had no idea of his inner turmoil. Matt had kept his emotions secret. Not long after this revelation, we moved back to Virginia. I had learned a valuable lesson again: Matt would not show his grief. He would be strong (his notion of strength, not mine). I would have to look deeper, even more than I already was, if I were to read that particular emotion in my youngest son.

When we got the call that their paternal grandmother was in the hospital, we immediately packed and set off for Illinois. Grandma had cancer, and it had been in remission for such a long time that we were caught off guard when it suddenly returned with a vengeance. She was in intensive care. There were tubes and ventilator noises. It must have been tremendously scary for both boys.

Matt did not want to enter the room. He stood by door, taking quick glances toward Grandma, and just as quickly turned away. Christopher, the weight of the world evident on his face, walked in without hesitation. I could see Matt's eyes follow his brother and could almost hear him thinking, *If Chris could do it, then I could do it,* and after a few moments, Matt followed him in. How utterly brave he was to go into that room with all its smells and sounds. But he did do it, because his brother did. He knew he was supposed to go in that awful room because Christopher showed him that Grandma was more important than the fear he felt.

This brings me to today and the reason behind this story. Our cat, Toulouse, died yesterday of feline leukemia. Christopher was a teenager when he found Toulouse, a yellow domestic kitten in a parking lot. When he brought him in, we were hit with the familiar line, "Can we keep him?" How could we not? Toulouse soon became Christopher's best buddy, and spent most of his time on his lap or at his computer. They were inseparable. Unfortunately, when Christopher grew up and bought a house, he couldn't take his best friend, his cat. He feared he would run away with the new surroundings and, knowing how well he was rooted to our home, decided to have us keep him.

Christopher's beloved cat instantly became Matt's favorite of our three. He nicknamed him Wildcat, and he loved him even more than he had before. This was his brother's cat, and he would be honored to take care of him. Matt continued to treat Toulouse like the royalty he was. Matt moved into Christopher's old room, and Toulouse kept his routine of spending much of his time hanging out his same room, only now with Matt.

We learned only a week ago that Toulouse had leukemia. The vet brought him back from the brink of death but explained to us there was nothing more to be done. We knew we would only have him for a short time. I explained this to Matt. Then yesterday Toulouse began having difficulty breathing. He was dying, and we had a choice—to let him struggle to the end or put him down. We chose the latter. Again, I saw the weight of the world on my oldest son's face. As time drew near to the appointment, I realized both my sons needed time away. I asked Christopher to please take Matt until it was over. Matt knew what was happening and that the time had come. He was relieved to go with his brother. Before he left, Matt got his camera and took a picture of his friend, his beloved pet, then patted his head gently and whispered good-bye. Christopher took Matt to town, and we took Toulouse on his final trip to the vet.

Christopher instinctively knew a diversion was needed. He took Matt to get something to eat and then to get a video game, the perfect detractor. When we had buried Toulouse, we called Christopher and they came back to the house. Matt poured his energy and attention to his new game. He needed to not think, not feel, not cry. His game helped him achieve these goals. Christopher, needing to absorb what had happened, spent a moment alone at the gravesite.

Today, I walked Matt out to the grave. He tensed up. I told him Toulouse was buried there, pointing to the large rock that covered the site. Matt took a step back. His eyes moist, he looked but could go no further. I told him that Christopher took a moment alone there yesterday and that whenever he needed to, he could do the same. The tension eased a bit. I told him I would talk with him when he was ready, and then I changed the subject. He instantly relaxed, grateful not to dwell on it. Matt still has not cried. He told me he will not. He is steadfast. He is doing exactly as Christopher. I am sure they will both cry eventually, probably alone and to themselves. It's very private, and the pain is overwhelming. The waves can only rise to the surface of thought a little at a time. I know from experience that memories of Toulouse will surface time and again, and sometimes tears will come and eventually, down the road, a smile. Neither will openly grieve in my presence anytime soon. Neither will want to discuss it, not for a long time.

I am glad I understand how my oldest deals with grief because it has allowed me to understand how Matt also deals with grief. If I didn't know and accept these variations on processing grief, I would worry about how it is affecting Matt, wonder why he didn't talk about it, wonder why there were no tears. If not for Christopher, I would not know how to help my autistic son. These are two very empathetic and deeply feeling young men. There is nothing wrong in how they deal with grief—we each have our own way. Matt's just happens to mirror his brother's. I know that being autistic does not mean that Matt cannot feel the pain of grief. On the contrary, he feels too deeply for words. It means that I will watch and wait and exercise patience. I will be ready for when it surfaces, and I know eventually we will talk, when the pain is not so intense. Months, maybe years from now, we will talk about this beautiful, wonderful cat and we will come to peace, all of us, in our own time.

For autistic and non-autistic alike, grief is the most over-whelming of emotions. Patience and understanding are required of those on the outside. We learn to wait and be ready to lift them up when grief tries to pull them down. As intense as it can be, we are all willing to accept the eventuality of grief. I know that I do because I want…no, crave, the experiences of love and joy.

Matt chooses to enjoy the wonderful lives that enter his and knowingly immerses himself in the warmth of their love—knowing grief is part of the deal. How amazing is that?

PUBERTY
BECOMING SELF-AWARE

MATT HAS CHANGED dramatically over the years. The changes really hit high gear when he entered puberty. As a child, Matt flapped his hands, enjoyed spinning toys, twirled, lacked speech and eye contact, lined up cars, and displayed "inappropriate laughter and tears." When speech did come, he used echolalia, the constant echoing back of something that was said to him. He hid under chairs and tables, behind furniture, had not learned bowel control, and ate only items from a very limited list of foods. He spent a lot of time in the safety of his room, away from others and noise. Yep, classically autistic behaviors. Yet as he got older, some of these behaviors began to fade, and other behaviors appeared...a state of constant change.

His confidence increased, and he began to interact with his family members a little bit more. Gone are the flapping of hands, the spinning of toys, the twirling, and the downward cast of the eyes. If he knows you, then he looks directly at you when speaking. If he doesn't, his eyes flicker away and back during the conversation, as if trying to gauge if it is safe. There's no echo in his speech patterns. If he doesn't understand, he'll produce an expression of confusion and say, "I don't know." His sense of humor is amazing, always ready to give comic relief. There's no hiding, no more lying on the ground in protest.

Strangely, as each classic autistic behavior slowly faded, so did his memory of that behavior. I didn't realize it until after it had already occurred several times. I would remind Matt of some event, and he could not recall it. Again, much later, I would ask, "Remember when you use to do...?" and again the reply would be a frustrated no. Matt's memory for data was still functioning, and at top speed. It was the emotional memory that was deteriorating. He could not remember certain things in his past—like twirling or shadow dancing. He couldn't remember ever having flapped his hands. When anyone brought these things up in his presence, or within hearing distance, he would push his mind to recall what they were talking about and could not find it in his memory.

Matt could remember trips and movies, and songs from the immediate past, but not a memory survived of his classically autistic self. He felt as if he had not lived prior to today. My son was in mourning of his own memories. I had to try and help him through this scary time, and I needed to tread carefully. I started slow, explaining to him that I too could no longer remember much about my days as a young child. I told him it was normal to let some things go. I then told him for the first time what autism was, adding that he was learning quickly and that he was doing very well and was getting better. Matt needed to hear it. It made sense. He was becoming aware that he was different, that his siblings acted like the people on TV and in the movies whereas he did not.

Matt entered puberty. He grew like a weed, his blond hair slowly turning a deep brown, his voice cracked then deepened. His outward appearance was obviously changing. Is it such a leap to think his mind was changing too? Do you remember your puberty years? Confusion sets in as to who you really are. You become self-aware. You look to your peers for clues on how to act, what to say, what to wear. You secretly believe your friends have the inside track on behavior and taste. You mirror your peers, trying to fit in. Matt relied on his siblings, mostly his older brother Christopher, to show him how to act and how to dress. He wanted to be just like him. He mirrored him as best he could. Where before I had picked out his clothes each day, Matt was now deciding these crucial elements himself, choosing items of clothing that he saw others his age wearing.

Could it be possible that the hormones flooding his brain during puberty actually enhanced a self-awareness that had been lurking beneath the surface? Was the loss of memory of who he related to the new connections the hormones initiated? I like to think of it as a pruning of the dendritic tree to allow room for new neural growth within the brain. The old connections to classically autistic behavior were being pruned, replaced by newer, stronger connections between the emotion and learning centers of his brain.

Over the years I have talked openly to Matt about his autism. We talked in private, secretly discussing changes in everything from brushing his teeth to how to answer a phone. He understood, and he tried to modify his behavior. I soon noticed that certain modifications to his behavior came shortly after our talks. He was changing, not because *I* wanted him to change, but because *he* wanted himself to change. It was Matt who expected himself to be perfect—a hold-over from his earlier days when perfection was everything.

Puberty, like everything else in autism, took longer than normal. Progress was slow but steady. Social interactions were still very difficult, and he hated that he was inept with the interactions in a group. Matt was in his early twenties when it all came to the surface. It was Thanksgiving, just after dinner, and we were setting up for the annual poker game. I heard Matt sobbing from his room, and my heart instantly ached. I went in and sat down. He waited for me to ask what was wrong then burst into tears as he replied in a desperate, heart-wrenching voice, "I'm different!" followed by "I hate my brain!" His eyes glanced toward the poker table. Matt had never played cards with us at Thanksgiving. He had never taken part in our family poker night—too much noise, too much sensory overload. He had always chosen the safety of his room. He had always been different. He didn't want to be different any longer, but he was unsure of how to change.

His sad eyes, his sobbing voice, and his gesture all screamed at me, "I want to play!" He had been watching our poker ritual from afar for years, and although he was always invited to play, he had always refused, declining in a polite "No thanks." Could this Thanksgiving bring a new response?

I asked, "Do you want to play poker?" To my surprise, he answered a resounding "Yes!" Smiling, my heartbeat racing, I led him to the den. Matt was greeted with high-fives and smiles all around. His siblings provided a flurry of encouraging remarks and funny quips, immediately putting him at ease.

That night, Matt learned to play poker. More importantly, Matt chose to interact with a very noisy group of people, learn something new, and take a leap into the unknown. He conversed (short and to the point), he played, he provided comic relief, and he dealt with the environmental onslaught of sights and sounds that had to be difficult to process. But he stayed. He had decided he wanted to and was determined to see it through. This was his family, completely enveloping him in their loving embrace, and Matt knew he was welcome among them. He was a part of something special.

At the age of twenty-two, Matt bravely chose to step out of the safety of his room into the unknown. Into a world he had only viewed from afar and dreamt of being a part of. He entered our world that night, and he never looked back. Tears came and silently ran down my cheeks, and I wiped them away and laughed at the next joke, the next silly comment, but silently I was welcoming my son.

Hello, Matt. We've been waiting for you.

IN AUTISM, A GAME
IS NOT JUST A GAME

WHAT WAS THE first game you ever played with your child? Most parents would probably say "peek-a-boo." It's hard to play peek-a-boo with an autistic child because it requires them to look at your face or into your eyes—something that is very difficult for them to do. One of the first games I played with my son Matt was airplane. I would swing him around in a circle, much to his delight—except Matt needed me to swing him facing away from me. Trying to engage my autistic son in a game was difficult. Instead, we would go for walks or stack blocks.

But stacking blocks is not a game. Real games require skill and attention to detail and someone wins and someone loses. Games in that regard didn't begin until much later. Back then I didn't know whether Matt would ever be able to join the rest of his family in playing a game, but I decided to keep my expectations high. Being autistic meant that Matt was a loner—he didn't seem to like to play games. I believe the social interactions were just too complex for him when he was little.

Then we bought our first video game. It makes perfect sense that he would be so attracted to them. After all, the games were dynamic and visually appealing, and he could play by himself. There are times when I have wondered if the real force behind his learning to read was the desire to know the rules, shortcuts, and to obtain all the bonus points offered in his video games.

Matt eagerly took on video games. He used this time to himself to practice moves and explore various strategies without someone watching him or, heaven forbid, interfering. Not only could he explore new worlds that were simple and organized, he could also put away the chaos of the real world. The complex and annoying sounds of family life emanating from the rest of the house were drowned out by the happy tunes of Mario Brothers and dinosaur screams of Jurassic Park. Video games didn't require him to interact with anyone else. I really think that the attraction of the video game went even deeper. I think it took the stress off his shoulders, the stress of being in a world he didn't understand, a place that scared him.

Matt began to talk at five years old and began the habit of thinking aloud. It was this outer monologue that provided me with clues to what he was thinking and opened a door into his thoughts and feelings. For example, listening to him talk to himself, I discovered he could pretend—something thought to be impossible for autistic children. I can remember many times just listening to him converse with the characters in his video games. I often wondered, "Why can Matt converse so easily with the animated characters of his games but not with me?" After spending hours watching and listening, I finally found my answer—Matt's imaginary conversations was his way of practicing speech without the fear of failure or any interruption of thought. It was safer. I found out years later that Matt carried a tremendous amount of fear. Fear of failure was 90 percent of it. Matt wanted to do everything perfectly, and when it was not, he would berate himself. His self-worth was tied intimately to his view of perfection.

Playing with another person may have appeared to be an easy transition, but it only came about after Matt had practiced conversing with his animated friends. His skill level was at the top, and he began to notice the behaviors and interactions of his hero, his older brother, Christopher. Matt found playing with his brother advantageous as he learned new skills. Matt would secretly watch his brother play a video game, but he was afraid to ask to play even though he wanted it so badly it hurt. On occasion, Christopher would see Matt spying on him and ask him to play. In the early years, whenever the opportunity arose to play with Matt, it was an unwritten rule in our family to allow him to win every time. This encouraged him to play with others more often and not only increased his confidence but also lessened his fear of interaction. Unfortunately, you just can't let them win indefinitely. Sooner or later they also have to learn how to lose. The era of the contest thus began.

Christopher was a fierce competitor at heart, and it wasn't long before the games took on the feel of Olympic competition. Matt had to fine-tune his skills in order to stay competitive, and he would play (practice) for hours almost every day. Even with such diligence, he had days when he lost in competition to his highly skilled brother. Losing was like a slap in the face to Matt back then. It inevitably brought tears and temper tantrums. Yet as much as I wanted peace and tranquility, I wanted to see progress even more. I would soothe his feelings and talk about it "just being a game," but Matt didn't understand. To him, losing was an assault on his very being. Losing made him feel inadequate, less of a person.

Christopher had been a good sport for the longest time, and it was time to let him prove himself a champion gamer also. It was important to let Christopher lose to use his skills just as it was important to let Matt figure out how to deal with losing. It felt like forever, but eventually Matt was able to accept the loss without the meltdown. To get through this tortuous time, I had to learn a very important lesson: losing was synonymous with imperfection in Matt's eyes.

Years later, when the meltdowns finally ceased, I could fully appreciate the magnitude of what he had endured. There are so many roadblocks with autism. Getting past this one—learning to lose—was one of the hardest. The worst part was witnessing his pain—the pain of discovering imperfection. To Matt, losing meant he was somehow less, and the blow to his self-worth was always heart-wrenching. There were many days when watching my autistic son pass through these excruciating stages tore my soul apart. Yet as difficult as it was on Matt, he never gave up. In doing so, he gained insight into himself. His worth as a person was not tied to his ability to win a game. A game is just a game. With an indomitable spirit, Matt pushed himself forward, kept making progress, and slowly turned away from the safety of complete solitude. Matt was determined to understand the complexities of winning and losing and, in so doing, found he could be part of our family's social interaction dynamics.

As the years went by, I watched Matt take part in bolder, more socially intensive games. He joined in for board games, swimming pool games, card games, and outdoor games. But the story doesn't end there. Just recently he jumped his last hurdle in the area of family games. Matt played flashlight tag with us for the very first time. Our family has played this game countless times over the years, ever since the children were all very young. The game is basically hide-and-seek after dark. Matt hates the dark.

In this game, the seeker gets a flashlight, and if they shine it on you and call your name, then you must go to "jail," a reserved area of the deck, until someone breaks you out by tagging you. Another area is reserved as base—if you make it to base, then you are free to rescue those in jail. It requires planning, blending in with shadows, knowing when to move very quickly and when to move slowly. To be good at this game, those in hiding must be willing to climb trees, lie under bushes, or belly crawl along the grass. Over the years, our children have gotten very good at this game. Matt, however, has never played. He would always stay indoors in the light of his room and play a video game while the rest of our family braved the darkness. The darkness is something that Matt still fears, even at twenty-eight years old. We have tried countless times to coax him out, but he would always decline, that is, until our twentieth wedding anniversary.

To celebrate our anniversary, we decided what we really wanted was family time. The kids are all grown-up, and getting the entire tribe together is almost impossible. My husband's two children (Jacob and Sarah) are both married. My oldest (Christopher) has his own house and a long-time girlfriend. Everyone is busy with home and work and responsibilities. Our request for family time was very specific—we would be playing one last game of flash-light tag. My husband and I are in our fifties, and I just can't see myself crawling on the ground or sprinting toward base for too many more years. Matt knew of our plans to play and waited for his invitation as usual. When I asked him if he wanted to play also, thoroughly expecting him to decline, I was surprised and delighted to hear "Yes!" as his reply.

The game got under way soon after dark. Matt became Christopher's partner to learn the ropes on both hiding and seek-ing. He hid well, he sought to free those trapped in jail, and he seemed to enjoy all of it.

All of it, that is, until he became the seeker. Christopher and Matt each had a flashlight and began collecting victims almost immediately. Unfortunately, Matt failed to capture me, and this upset up him tremendously. He marched back to the house and went to his room. I went in to speak with him. I reminded him that it was just a game, that it was just for fun, and that he was an adult. Matt takes pride in being an adult and hearing me refer to him as an adult immediately got his attention. Matt is deter-mined to live independently, and he knows from our many con-versations that he must act like an adult to live as an adult. He looked directly into my eyes as I reminded him that on occasion I win at Wii Sports and he tells me "Good job, Momma." For me to evade detection in a game of flashlight tag was no different.

Matt thought about this for a minute. I could see the wheels turning as he looked at me and could actually tell the exact moment he made the connection to the other games he had played. When it clicked, a smile returned to his face, and he hugged me. Matt understood—flashlight tag was just a game, nothing more. It was not an insult to his intelligence or to his self-worth. He was not less simply because he couldn't find me in a silly game. We both returned to the group and continued to play long into the night. Matt seemed to put more life into his game; he laughed more and interacted more. He obviously enjoyed himself much more after our short talk. The joy he felt was because the fear of failure had been lifted from him. He felt good about himself—he knew he was not less.

Games are not just games to the autistic child. To them they are a chaotic collection of mysterious mannerisms, facial expressions, voice fluctuations, gestures, and emotions that have to be unraveled slowly and meticulously to be understood. Maybe other autistic children are like Matt in that they view their performance in a game as a measure of their own self-worth. Matt knows he is autistic and that it makes him different but that doesn't mean he has to feel as if he is less. Through games Matt has learned to cope with disappointment. Losing no longer means failure or imperfection. It just means it's someone else's turn to win. I feel honored to have taken this journey with him, knowing I have the luxury of looking back to see just how far he has come. This amazing young man is the most courageous person I have ever known. It took something deep inside him, pushing him hard, to try to understand the mysteries and complexities of social interaction. I know in my heart that it has been Matt's determination and courage—not mine—that allowed each transition to transpire. From learning to converse to overcoming fear of failure, games have been an integral part of Matt's social development.

MAKING THE DECISION
FOR GUARDIANSHIP

As I sit at my computer, I can tell a beautiful fall is just around the corner. The leaves are just waiting to turn bright shades of yellow and orange, and the nights are about to get cooler—I can smell it. I look forward to the fall—mostly.

This fall there are added events. It just happens that this year we will once again go to the polls to vote for the candidate that best reflects our hopes for the future. Matt loves politics and will eagerly go with me to the polls to vote, but Matt's vote doesn't count. I have yet to tell him because it breaks my heart. Matt, my wonderful twenty-six-year-old son, was deemed legally incompetent at the age of eighteen, and that means he is not eligible to cast his own ballot. How do I tell him that in this land of freedom, equality, and diversity, his voice will not be heard?

It hits me twice as hard this year because it is time again for me to complete the Guardian's Annual Report. Filling out the report is not difficult, but the weight of it on my soul can be very difficult indeed.

In order to become the legal guardian and conservator for my autistic son, the court had to first find him incompetent to manage his own affairs. It was (and still is) a very emotional process. It is something that I had to choose to initiate because I knew Matt needed me to do it, but that doesn't mean I took it in stride. It literally took years of thoughtful contemplation to even begin the legal process. I tried my best to weigh the consequences for both obtaining guardianship and not pursuing it at all. Unfortunately, each comparison always pointed toward the "must get it done" side of the argument. No matter what people might tell you, having your child deemed legally incompetent is neither an easy route nor a desired one.

I felt all those hopes and dreams in the back of my mind—the ones where I pictured my son being able to make it on his own one day—begin to disappear as I put pen to paper and signed that one official document. I realized in an instant, before the ink even had a chance to dry, that this beautiful mind, this wonderful young man that is my son, would never be like so many other autistic people—people like Temple Grandin who have made it on their own. He would never be completely free to make his own decisions every day, or have full independence to live the life he chose to have.

It is not something to be taken lightly, the role of guardian, and yet I can see very clearly that it could be easily abused. *Guardianship* does not mean dictatorship—it means protector. My son needs me for some things—I accept that and Matt accepts that—but I also need to allow him as much independence as possible. The hard part is figuring out at what point my role as his guardian begins and ends? To me, it's like chasing shadows across the lawn as the sun and clouds move across the sky. Just when you think you have it all figured out, the light shifts. The shadows can either become a deeper shade or become so thin as to let small beams of light poke through.

As Matt's guardian, it never ends, this shifting of responsibility. Even as an adult, Matt's autism is in flux. I have to remind myself that just because there are some things he can't do now, that doesn't mean he may not be able to do them next year, or the year after, or even ten years from now.

I knew Matt needed me to help him after the age of eighteen, as he was still in high school with graduation coming up quickly. Without guardianship, Matt would've refused to be given speech therapy, would have thrown away his IEP, and never would have fought the school system over the end of course exam in English. He needed that extra writing time and to have his exam read to him. Without guardianship, Matt would not have graduated number four in his class that year—and probably would not have graduated at all. Not because he didn't want those things, but because he would not have understood the implications for not having an IEP.

Matt can't communicate like you or I; he can't tell you his problems, his fears, his confusion, can't foresee the consequences of his actions; and he can't do finances. The worst part for him of course is the difficulty talking to people. Please understand, Matt *can't*, not *won't*. He is learning every day, and because we have a special type of communication between us, I can help him. Communication is at the heart of his "can't." As we work on communication and as his ability to speak to other people improves, I know some of those *can't* items will change to *can*. I know this. I have watched it happen many, many times before. It takes time and teaching and love.

My role as Matt's guardian is one I take very seriously. I am his mother, and as his mother, I shower him with love, acceptance, and opportunity to be all he can. I am his best friend and his shoulder to cry on. As his guardian, I am his teacher, his mentor, his financial officer, his personal health-care professional, his cruise ship director, and his drill sergeant. The roles overlap quite often, I assure you. So as another fall arrives and I fill out another Guardian's Annual Report, I think of my son's future. I still have dreams of independence, but they are not as pristine as they once were. Matt's independence will be on a sliding scale between what he can really achieve and what he cannot *yet* achieve. I know I will continue to teach him every little thing I can think of, and we will tackle another year one day at a time.

He will again go with me to the polls on voting day as he has always done, and again he will walk beside me as we go behind the curtain to vote. I know Matt is not incompetent on politics and is actually very aware of which candidate has his best interests at heart. And again, I know I will not tell him that his freedom to vote as a US citizen has been stripped from him.

Instead, like on every Election day within the past decade and a half, I will give my son the voting pen and he will mark the ballot. As his guardian, I am his voice, and through me his voice will be heard because on voting day Matt is my right hand—the one that holds the pen. As his guardian, I will continue to protect him and will share my freedoms with him always, until that day—soon, I hope—when he can have his own freedoms returned.

HOME IS WHERE
HIS HEART IS...

SOMETIMES WITH AUTISM, a simple conversation can suddenly reach down into your heart and change your life and your future path forever. Like many of you, we have been experiencing hard times with this great recession, and financially we have come to a crossroads. Do we stay where we are, or do we move in hopes of securing a better future financially? It's been a roller coaster of a ride. We have lived in our home for twenty-four years (except for a brief attempt at job security on the other side of the country), and we have met and overcome our family challenges right here...in this home...in these beautiful mountains of Virginia. This is where our children were raised, educated, fell in love, and moved into their own homes, and this is where our youngest, Matt, has fought his many battles with autism.

It's important to have the financial security to provide a good life for Matt. Sometimes the emotional cost was overlooked, as in that last move to Arizona. Recently, I have been at war with myself over the direction our future should take...*again*. Do we sell our home, move to the city, and leave this wonderful place? Do we?

I decided about six months ago that in order to fulfill my job as Matt's caretaker, guardian, conservator, and mom, I would do whatever it took to make sure he was happy and his dreams of living independently became a reality. Regardless of the emotional attachment to this home, my job, my friends, and our other children, I would do whatever Matt needed me to do. Matt has worked so hard to achieve his ultimate goal of independence that I would not let him fall. I will always be his cheering section, his voice, his champion. I will see him reach his ultimate goal and neither hell nor high water would deter me from it. I would do whatever Matt needed me to do—just as I always have.

But Matt is not a child anymore, and independence is not just the ability to live alone, but also to make decisions that affect his own life. What is best for Matt? Do I decide for him? So when the possibility of a new job arose out of state, I had to really think things through.

My husband is on contract, but unfortunately, contracts are short and sporadic. He needs full-time security. A job within driving distance would be the perfect solution, but the great recession has made that possibility iffy. I also need a full-time job now, both to pay our bills and to help my son obtain his dream. Moving to a neighboring state could actually take care of both. There are jobs there for both my husband and myself, and in addition, a big city would have better services, buses, concerts, museums, and shopping that could enhance my son's life.

I convinced myself that for Matt, moving was best. Personally, I love it right where I am. I am willing to try and ride out the recession, wait for the right job, hold on to my own dreams of living in these beautiful mountains. Unfortunately, that may not be possible as we have been holding on now for five years and our financial resources are all dried up. Moving to secure full-time employment might be in all our best interests, and North Carolina has been tempting us with the possibility of jobs and resources. It seemed that North Carolina could be our future path. I thought maybe it was where God meant for us to go.

What I hadn't yet done was ask Matt what he wanted. What were his thoughts on this dilemma? It's not easy pulling thoughts from Matt's mind. It is a complex interaction that must be very carefully choreographed. Although he is highly intelligent, loving, funny, and talented, he is not a conversationalist. Matt is a twenty-eight-year-old man of few words. Conversations are mostly one-sided, with me doing most of the talking. Matt has always answered in sentences that are always either black or white. There are no gray areas to his replies or requests. I love that about my son, but I also had to work hard for many years to perfect my role in a conversation with him. I had to learn how to ask a question just right, how to present a problem based upon facts, how to explain emotions so he could understand the entire complex situation.

I also had to learn to listen to my son. His words, his body gesture, his facial expressions, his tone of voice—all had a part to play in his replies. Listening to Matt requires reading every aspect of his being. And so it was that one day a few years back, I sat down with my autistic son and presented the dilemma of our future path to him, in black and white. I gave him the good points and bad for each path, the big city or the small mountain town in Virginia. I was careful not to allow my own emotions to sway the decision. I was careful to be honest about the good points and the bad. I wanted his opinion, not a reflection of my own desires. I spoke directly, presented the facts, and assured him we would do what he wanted. I stressed to him that he was a full-grown man and his opinion counted. A period of silence followed.

I was totally convinced he would choose the big city. Matt loves North Carolina. We had visited the area many times, and he loved it. He knew the main roads, the locations of the museums, shopping, and other attractions and even stayed in an apartment there for several weeks with my husband while he was on contract. I prepared myself for a future move and the pain of leaving this beautiful place and all its memories. It was his decision, and I would go wherever Matt needed me to go.

I waited for his reply and found myself holding my breath. I just knew my life was about to change and a new path would be set before me—I hoped I was ready to move and start our life again in a new place.

When he spoke, he did so directly at me. His smiling face made me realize he was sure of his decision. His body was relaxed, his voice light. Matt had been waiting to be asked for a very long time. He now had his chance to enter the conversation and would speak his mind.

"I want to live in *my* mountains. I want to ride my bike to the stores and to see the fireworks from the elementary school on the Fourth of July. My brother will take me to the county fair, and we will climb the rock wall, eat lunch, and shop at the bookstore in Roanoke. You will stay with me at my new apartment sometimes, and sometimes I will stay with you. I will have an apartment in my Appalachia."

I sat stunned. No museums, no big stores, no buses, and he didn't care. The Appalachian Mountains are his home and his life, and they had a stronger hold on him than I realized. He must have thought about this for a long time as he spoke of plans on how his future summers would be, where he would go, and who he would spend time with. Our future path had just been set in stone—Matt would attempt his independence right here in our own little corner of the world. His words reached down into my heart, and suddenly I knew my future path. Suddenly, it didn't matter how long we would continue to fight to stay in our home, where the jobs were, or where Matt would have better resources.

At once I knew the only thing that mattered was the fulfilling of a dream, and my dreams and my son's dreams were one and the same.

Suddenly I realized, without a doubt, that we *would* follow our dreams. My joy is overwhelming. My resolve is great. I will see my son's dreams come to fruition right here in my own Blue Ridge Mountains of Virginia, and nothing, not even the lure of more money, can deter me from making that happen. Nothing. Thank you, Matt.

YES, AN AUTISTIC CHILD CAN PRETEND

MATT HAS ALWAYS loved concerts and plays. Sarah, his stepsister, was in quite a few of these events starting in middle school. We recorded her first play, and Matt would watch the video tape over and over (and over and over). He absolutely loved the idea of pretending to be someone else. It is interesting to note that one of the behaviors listed in describing autism is "no pretend play," but this is just another one of those behaviors that seem to be in place only in the early years—it is not set in stone. The autism brain has a lag phase, when many neurotypical behaviors are simply put on hold. In Matt's case, it took years to learn to pretend, but once he began, he never stopped. One of the events important to learning to pretend came in watching Sarah pretend to be someone else, in front of an audience, and the audience laughed! This must have shown Matt that pretending was not only acceptable, it was also fun. He watched that video daily—and for years!

Pretending to be someone else became part of his ritual. In playing a video game, he would pretend to be in the action along with the animated participants, memorizing dialogue as if he were memorizing the lines of a play. As he grew older, he learned to add his own lines, ad lib according to the situation occurring on the video screen. This really took off when Matt became a member of the OM team for Sheffey Elementary. OM, or Odyssey of the Mind, was an academic competition that included putting on skits. Matt found himself a member of a team that pretended. He loved it. He found the skits to be funny, and when Matt found something funny, you knew it—his laugh was (and still is) a very deep, heartfelt emotion bubbling up from his very soul, and it was (and still is) very contagious.

He still lacked the ability to speak fluently, and this lent to trouble reciting his lines, not with his ability to memorize, only in his actual ability to speak. Matt had difficulty with pronunciation and grammar, and his roles in each skit were usually more active and less talk. He loved it. Not having to speak took away the stress of being different. He never seemed uncomfortable performing to large groups of strangers. This was most likely due to the closeness of his team, his ability to keep focused on them, and his ability to tune out the rest.

Matt eventually got too old to be in OM, and his grammar and pronunciation were still far from perfect, hindering any possibility in being in the plays at the high school level. Yet Matt continued to pretend with his video games and with his favorite movies. It was during this time that I started teaching—in a different high school. I started taking Matt to see the spring play each year. He loved them! He even videotaped the play and gave copies to the cast. Each of the students from the play would meet Matt and shake his hand. That small gesture solidified them into his memory. He felt accepted—and normal. My students have always been very good with Matt.

Matt still pretends. Each video game he plays he puts himself into the starring role, memorizing dialogue and even adding his own remarks where appropriate. The act of pretending has helped advance his speech. His voice is now much clearer, he still has a small stutter when he can't find just the right word and still uses an "umm" before a long sentence, possibly his way of organizing his thoughts before speaking.

Pretending has also given Matt a way to be normal. He can enter any fictitious world and be "the man." He uses the pretend play as a way to practice interactions, hone conversation skills, and be someone who is not autistic, even if it is only for a few hours each day.

Pretending. It is a simple behavioral stage that all children go through. For the autistic child, pretending must be learned, just as they learn every other behavior, by practice and observation. After Matt saw his first play, Sarah's play, he was hooked. The days, months, and even years of listening to her play on tape drove us crazy. Yet now, years and years later, I can look back and see the importance of that play. It was a beginning. Matt knew if Sarah could do it that he could do it. He knew it was acceptable and normal. He knew it was fun and entertaining.

Matt's autism-cloud may have hindered his interaction and speech abilities, but his natural instincts showed him the way out from under that cloud. Pretending is definitely one of the wonderfully great methods he used to light his path.

LATE TO BED, LATE TO RISE

I HAVE INSOMNIA on occasion, and after tossing and turning for hours, I will finally give up and just get out of bed. I usually get up at 4:30 a.m., but on nights when I can't sleep, my resignation usually sets in around 2:00 to 3:00 a.m. Regardless of the day of the week, whenever I have insomnia, I can walk out of my room and give my son Matt a hug. He's still up and he's always happy to see me. For Matt, being up all night is part of who he is. Matt is a true night owl.

Most parents get up in the morning, wake the kids for school, and everyone starts their day together. For the entire duration of Matt's school years, getting him up and going was a real chore. Tears and anger greeted me each morning and again most nights when I put him to bed. Most of this was due to Matt's fear of the dark. He has required a light in order to sleep since autism set in at age two. When Matt graduated from high school, I allowed him to choose his own schedule. It really came as no surprise that he chose to be up all night and only head to bed as the first rays of sunlight began to appear each morning.

His new schedule was not a problem for us as my husband and I have worked opposite shifts for most of our marriage. My husband worked nights and I worked days. Someone was always home with Matt. Matt's night-owl schedule didn't even faze us as Matt slept when Tom slept and got up when Tom got up. When he awoke, he spent the afternoon and evenings alternating between interacting with us and doing things on his own. When late evening came, I would go to bed, my husband to work, and Matt would revel in his time alone in a quiet house. This wasn't surprising either because I knew how much constant sounds and commotion annoyed him.

When he was still in school, it was difficult for him to be subjected to noise and constant activity all day. Is it any wonder then that his first decision as a new graduate was to choose a schedule that would lessen the assault of noise on his senses? I thought his new schedule would last a month and he would finally get into a more "normal" schedule—but it became clear after that first month that Matt was enjoying his freedom and his nighttime "king of the house" status too much to ever willingly give it up. I tried bribing him, cajoling him, and even forced the issue a few times before I realized that it was I who was wrong in trying to change him.

Over time I began to see that his new schedule brought with it some very cool perks—like happiness and mental focus. Matt is always in a good mood now. It is obvious that his stress level is very low, which allows him to focus on learning and creativity. He watches science DVDs and various ones on history. He draws, listens to his music, reads, and can think freely without interruption. His level of communication has been enhanced, and he's more willing to interact during his afternoons and evenings with us. His fears are abating. He is always willing to go somewhere, do something, even if he has never done that particular activity before. Matt obviously loves life.

Everyone has a biological rhythm set just for them, but unfortunately most people must adhere to the cultural norms in order to work to pay the bills and put food on the table. But if you could pick your schedule, wouldn't it be different from what you do now? At twenty-six years old, Matt had been my night owl for seven years. I asked him to give me a few reasons as to why he liked his schedule so much. He listed them for me. As I listened, I understood completely. Basically, it boils down to three simple reasons:

THE HOUSE IS QUIET

The dogs are sleeping, the phone doesn't ring, there's no traffic zooming past the house, no airplanes skimming the treetops, and no one comes to the door. The only noises in the house are noises of his own making: his music, his TV, his video games.

HE IS IN CHARGE

No one is telling him what to do. He feels more like an adult, more "normal" as everything he does is his choice. He can read books on his Kindle or one of his many paperbacks without interruption, and Matt reads a lot.

THE LIGHTS ARE ON

Darkness is terribly frightening, and the lights keep the darkness at bay while his activities allow him to not think about the darkness outside. He sleeps only after the sunrise—when the darkness has again been beaten back to simple shadows and the light of dawn signals the safety of a new day.

My husband and I and Matt each have our own schedule to this day, and amazingly, they don't conflict. Each of us has our quiet time, our busy time, and our family time. I use the mornings when I am off work to clean house, do finances, grade papers, or even write. I am now as spoiled in my routine as Matt is in his. As you are probably aware, time to oneself while your kids are young is almost impossible. What I have now is a very different life, and I will admit it—I like it. I am happier too.

I can't even come up with a good reason anymore as to why Matt should be forced to abide by my schedule. It's not like he's in need of supervision. He's old enough to handle responsibility pretty well. If he needs me, he knows where I am and can come get me, but he rarely needs me. We still eat meals together and have time to share stories or watch TV, or go somewhere together every day, so it's not like he doesn't interact. On days when I have to take him to the dentist in the morning (or to some other appointment), I warn him in advance that he will need to get up early, and he does so without argument or complaint. Of course, he doesn't go to bed much earlier the night before (it's a darkness thing), so he just survives on less sleep for a day.

Normally, Matt gets up every afternoon and immediately does his chores (without me asking). He fixes his own meals as I fix ours. He takes great pride in his independence, and his schedule reinforces that pride each and every day. Most importantly, he has learned to accept who he is. All children eventually grow up and find their niche in life, and I am confident that Matt will be successful in his own quest. I know he doesn't fret about the fact that he is different anymore. He likes himself. He is confident. His choice to be a night owl was the right one for him. It was me who had to learn to bend and be more flexible.

As parents, we feel great pride when our children come to the point where they are happy in their own skin. I am very proud of my son. It is apparent to me now that over the last decade he has learned much about himself through introspection during those quiet wee hours of the morning. Matt is fully aware that his autism makes him different, and yet he is happy with who he is and doesn't think about it much.

I am reminded of an interview with Temple Grandin when she was asked if she wanted to be cured. Her reply was no; she was happy with whom she was and didn't see the need to have to be like everyone else. Matt is on that road of self-acceptance and independence. He knows he has several goals to reach, and each of those goals require him to find a way to lessen the effect his autism has on his ability to communicate effectively with others.

Yet even his awareness of his communication deficits does not change the fact that he is not interested in being anyone but who he is.

Out of curiosity I asked him, "Matt, if there were a cure for autism, would you want to be cured?" He scrunched his face as if I had just insulted him and replied with a resounding, "No!"

My heart leapt unexpectedly. I am not only thrilled Matt has found self-acceptance, I am also convinced it was a direct result of his decision to be a night owl, a decision that led directly to lower stress and a clearer mind and introspection. What is really mind blowing is that none of it could've happened if I had not been willing to bend. If I had pushed him to conform to a normal "early to bed, early to rise" type of schedule, would he be so confident and happy now? I never would have guessed that "late to bed, late to rise" would prove to be such a cornerstone of personal development.

WHOSE ROCK ARE YOU?

SEVERAL DAYS AGO Matt came to give me my morning hug, and upon seeing him a red flag went up. Matt looked "peaked." Peaked (peek-ed) is an expression that was used by my grandmother many years ago to describe a pale not-quite-well state of health. I noticed his eyes were puffy and his face a bit swollen and pale in conjunction with his usual morning smile. My immediate summation was that Matt had either been crying or was ill.

"Are you okay?" I inquired gently. "I'm fine," his usual reply, even when sick. "You don't look like you feel very well," I added. I felt his forehead, and it was warm. "Your eyes are puffy. Does your face hurt?" I continued as I pressed gently on his face above his sinuses.

"Oh?" he said quizzically. Matt was trying to figure out what I wanted. At the same time I was trying to figure out what was wrong with him. Matt showed no response to my pressing his sinuses. I looked in his throat and saw it to be red and his tonsils slightly swollen. Nothing severe, thank goodness. There was just enough redness to signal to me that Matt was indeed fighting some nasty little virus (how dare a virus have the audacity to come into our home!).

For the next few days, Matt took a decongestant and took it easy. The decongestant messed with his sleep patterns, and he was up for more hours than usual, but he acted okay, and he ate fine. I'm the one that was on edge. I felt myself under a constant state of alert. You see, Matt's autism has always prevented him from distinguishing pain and illness from normal functioning. I can't say with any certainty that he can't feel pain, but he definitely has trouble determining whether his pain or discomfort is worth mentioning.

When Matt was two and a half years old, he was hit on the chin by a swing, which resulted in a deep cut that bled terribly. It upset Matt that a red liquid was emerging on his face, but he never showed a response to the actual pain he must have had. That was the first sign of his sensory problems. Since then, he has had pneumonia and never coughed, ear infections where the only indicator was an occasional swipe across the ear with his hand (as if to brush it away), a urinary tract infection where the only symptom was the smell, as well as other illness and injuries. For each occurrence, I have always relied on investigation and deductive reasoning, and it's always a bit scary.

When he was about eight years old, I noticed he had an occasional cough and a low-grade fever. In addition, he lost his appetite and slept more. Matt, to my mind, was very sick. I reasoned that anything that caused him to deviate from his normal routine had to be serious. The doctor did a quick listen to his chest and declared it the flu and sent us home.

I was not convinced. I sensed something was terribly wrong—I just knew it. When we left his office, instead of going home, we went directly to another doctor's office. This doctor decided to do an x-ray, mostly at my insistence. The x-ray showed one of Matt's lungs to be completely full, and the other nearly full. Matt had a severe case of double pneumonia, for which he was immediately admitted to the hospital, put on IVs and antibiotics and breathing treatments. While we were there, his first doctor stopped in to apologize. He had just learned a valuable lesson about listening to a mother of an autistic child.

Memories of other instances have been popping up all day. This latest virus has me wondering how I will ever allow Matt to live on his own. How can he when he could get severely sick and not tell a soul? How could I sleep at night wondering how he is and knowing that if I call him and ask, he will always say, "I'm fine." Planning his life requires taking everything I know about Matt and working on every area of concern in a way he can respond to. This is no easy task. I know I must really work with Matt to express himself, especially when it comes to both pain and illness. In addition, I have to constantly try to foresee as many obstacles as possible in order to address them early. The scary part is...what if I fail?

I know I am responsible for this very special human being for the rest of my life, and I must admit there are days when I wonder if I am up to it. Am I doing right by my son? Am I giving him what he needs? Am I doing everything I need to? There's nothing like the sick feeling of failure when it comes to your child (don't all parents have days like that?). The sudden fear for my son, the panic of "what if," consumed my thoughts for most of the day. Thank goodness it has passed and I am feeling stronger again. Life goes on. You can be sure I have now added "telling someone you're sick" to the list of goals Matt must reach before he can live on his own.

Make no mistake, Matt will live independently someday. But realize too that achieving all the goals is an awesome and sometimes overwhelming task. I have my times of weakness, days when I feel so incompetent as his caretaker, his friend, and his teacher. Days when I need some gentle support to get me through.

It's a hard road, being the parent of an autistic child, but one I will gladly travel with my son Matt and my husband Tom. Only the parents of an autistic child know—really know—what it is like. On those scary, panic-stricken days, support is everything.

So this week I have a request. If you know a parent of an autistic child (if you're reading this, then you probably do), give them some praise and possibly a shoulder to cry on. Let them know that you are aware that what they face is a lifelong journey and that the stress can sometimes be overwhelming. Help them stay on their road and focused toward the future. I get my support from Tom. He's my rock. Thank you, sweetheart.

The big question is, whose rock are you?

IN THE BATTLE OF TEXTURES AND TACTILE SENSATIONS, NOTHING BEATS DESIRE

SENSATION—WHETHER VISUAL, AUDITORY, or tactile—can be difficult for the autistic individual. Overcoming the onslaught, dealing with the sensations, and figuring out how to interact in an environment filled with these uncomfortable and sometimes overwhelming stimuli are a daily ritual for many autistic children. Over the years, my son has learned not only how to accept them, but also figured out how to lessen the impact. Over the years I have watched him learn and grow, and just like every child, on the spectrum or not, he continues to learn how to interact in a complex world. How much of his success can be directly related to his *desire* to interact with his environment?

For example, this past month we carved pumpkins for Halloween. Now Matt has made drawings on pumpkins before, has even tried carving before, but this year he did it all. From cutting the cap to cleaning out the goo to creating a design to carving, Matt did it all. While all of these things required interaction and creativity, I am most impressed with his ability to think through a problem—more specifically, a sensory problem—and come up with a solution all by himself. Watching him I became convinced that his desire to succeed outweighed the obstacles his autism placed before him.

First, I must give you a bit of background on Matt's specific sensory issues. From age two, his childhood was impacted by sensory issues. Lights were too bright, textures were too overpowering, sounds were too loud, smells and tastes were too strong. Over the years he has learned to dim the lights, muffle the sounds, taste something new in minute bites, and overcome his aversion to certain textures. Matt has increased his threshold for all of these things, being much more capable now than he was as a child to interact in an environment filled with sensory assaults. He can shoot targets as long as he wears ear protection, can enjoy a get-together in a brightly lit room, and has learned which foods are enjoyable and which ones are not worth even tasting because he has learned that smell and taste go together. The one sensory area that he continues to battle on a regular basis has been tactile. Some textures still feel too awful to put up with.

For example, Matt doesn't wear socks...ever. Socks suffocate his feet. It doesn't matter how cold it gets, Matt will put his shoes on without having first put on socks. When I have questioned him on this over the years, he generally gives the same reply: a wrinkled nose, a disgusted face, and "no thanks." It's obvious. Something about the feel of socks does not mesh with the sensation it makes on his skin. I haven't bought him socks in many years. I finally learned to accept that my son will never wear socks.

But socks are not the only problem. Certain shirts can't be worn, nothing with buttons or snaps or collars. Coats require zippers. Shorts are preferred over long pants. Long pants are acceptable only under certain circumstances. For instance, he will wear them only if it is so cold that he actually *has* to.

In contrast, some textures are wonderful. Matt likes the softness of his kitty's fur and will pet her lovingly. He is not so fond of dog fur, which is coarse (dogs are bigger and louder too, so there's more to it than just texture). He prefers baby animals, but all animals seem to have a piece of his heart. Kittens and puppies are even hold-able. Matt will actually put his face close to their face and snuggle briefly. But domesticated animals are not the only ones in his life. This past summer we rescued a pair of hatchling brown thrashers. We had them for several weeks, feeding them and walking them through flight school and bug hunting every day. What I found amazing was that Matt allowed these wild birds to sit in the palm of his hand and even latch on to a finger to perch. After that first experience, he knew full well the bird's feet were cold and the talons sharp, yet he was still eager to do it again and again. It was obvious his desire to pet the bird and hold it was stronger than the tactile sensation that came with it.

He really enjoys the petting zoo at the fair too and will hand-feed the adult emu, the zebu, and the llama, leaving me in awe as he feels the forceful peck of the emu and the wet, leathery lips of the zebu and llama as they lap at his palm. I remember when just holding the seed in his hand was a major accomplishment. Those early years of struggle and tears were met with an ever-increasing determination to succeed, fueled by a deeper, more powerful emotion—desire. Now Matt can even feed an Oreo cookie to a wild pony while on a day hike of the Appalachian Trail. The ponies are large and can be quite intimidating, but he fights any fears for the opportunity to interact with such a beautiful creature. The resulting smile says it all. I ask myself, "Is it desire that trumps tactile aversion? Does he find it within himself to overcome the uncomfortable sensations simply out of a deeper desire to experience a particular interaction?" It seems so…at least to me. I think maybe Matt has learned how to submit himself to certain textures and increase his threshold to certain sensations, because the desire to experience that specific interaction is just too great to ignore.

What about food? Matt enjoys finger foods, like pizza, corn on the cob, fries, and Tater Tots. He picked out these foods as a child and generally hasn't changed his diet much over the years. Some foods require eating utensils—pudding, ice cream, cake, peas, and broccoli. He would rather not use a spoon or fork, but I guess the taste is worth the uncomfortable feel of silverware in his mouth. Those few I listed are the only ones he will use silverware for (some things haven't changed much over the years, and I seriously don't think it's the feel of the utensil in his hand; I think it's the feel of it on his tongue).

Over the years, Matt has learned to touch and to deal with the sensations that touch can produce. And this leads us back to the recent Halloween pumpkin carving and the joy of witnessing another wonderful moment when he not only battled the unwanted sensation but used critical thinking to solve the problem of how to avoid it. This year my husband Tom, Matt, and I worked on pumpkins, all with a *Great Pumpkin* theme—Matt's favorite Halloween show. In the course of creating our pumpkins, I watched my son tackle one of the worst tactile sensations of his life.

I am talking about pumpkin goo, that slimy mess of seeds, vegetable fiber, and juice that must be removed from the pumpkin prior to carving. Matt watched his daddy remove the top of a pumpkin and start scooping out the nasty goo. Matt removed the top from his own pumpkin and slowly put his hand inside. A grimace washed over his face as he timidly pulled out a small bit, flung it on the newspaper, and hurriedly wiped his hand on a towel. Amazingly, he put his hand back in and repeated the process over and over, each time making a face that screamed "Yuck!" Determined to do this all himself, Matt submitted his entire being to the feel of pumpkin goo—a major accomplishment.

But that's not the whole story. Unfortunately, he couldn't finish the project that night, nor the next night, or the one after.
Sometimes other things just get in the way of a very cool project,
and that is what happened here. It was days later when there
was actually time to resume the great pumpkin carving of 2012.
By then however the pumpkin had begun to go bad. Having sat
in the warmth of his room, it had already begun to mold. The
pumpkin would have to be tossed and the project begun again
with a new pumpkin.

We all sat at the kitchen counter drawing our designs on our
pumpkins, each with a Snoopy motif. Then one by one we each
removed the top and started the removal of the goo. Matt opened
his pumpkin and stared inside. A look of disapproval emerged
on his face as he contemplated. A look of "Oh, not again!" slowly
emerged on his face. Then replacing this look was a new one, a
"wheels turning" type of look. Matt was working it out in his

head. Then he looked up at Tom and me and announced in a strong and forceful tone, "I need plastic gloves!"

Tom and I looked at each other for just a second, with smiles on our faces. We replied almost in unison, "That's a great idea!" Tom hunted and found a pair of blue nitrile gloves and handed them to Matt, who slipped them on like he had been using them his whole life, and happily proceeded in removing all the nasty goo. It was obvious that a feeling of empowerment had welled up within him. This generated a boost of energy that fueled his determination to get the job done. He flew through the chore so quickly that he finished before me, even though I had started first. Upon finishing, he removed the gloves with a "Ha!" and went to work on the desired carving of his much-loved Snoopy.

Triumphant and proud, Matt announced he was done, mission accomplished, the foe beaten. Matt, exceedingly pleased with both himself and his work, proudly displayed the finished project. As he walked to his room to engage in some much-needed video game time, I noted he stood taller, his shoulders back, his gait strong and confident. This was not just because he had *carved* a pumpkin—this was because he had figured out a way to *beat* the pumpkin.

I am sure now that it is desire that trumps sensation. I am confident that what I have seen over the years as Matt has taken on all those overwhelming sensations and forced himself to deal with the uncomfortable and sometimes painful stimuli, is one of determination, a strength of will fueled by sheer desire. By raising the threshold of sensation to new heights simply by a deep longing to interact with his environment, Matt is slaying dragons, the dragons of his autism. Desire, after all, is a powerful motivator. Autism forced him to deal with things you and I can only imagine, and Matt fights his autism every single day. He hates his autism, and he desires something more. He wants a regular life, an independent life, one where autism does not rule him, a life where he rules his autism. From the looks of it, his desire is his most powerful weapon in his ongoing battle to slay the negative aspects of his autism. I know I will never underestimate the power of sheer desire in overcoming the obstacles autism has placed before him. I have witnessed both his determination and his willpower. I have seen the courage that emerges when desire is more overwhelming than fear, more overwhelming than pain.

I understand now. I have been a witness to the slaying of dragons, and I am in awe.

IT'S HOT

DOESN'T A NICE dip in the hot tub sound great? My back is stiff and aching, and I find the hot water and strong jets are just what I need when the weather turns cool. I ask Matt if he wants to get in with Tom and me. Sometimes the answer is yes, but more often than not the answer is no. Matt loves water—always has. So why would he not want to get in the hot tub? Very simply, Matt is very sensitive to environmental stimuli. Included in this category are bright lights, loud sounds, strong odors, certain textures, certain tastes, and drastic temperature changes. At one point, when he was very young, all of these stimuli played a major role in his everyday life. Over the years he became more interactive with his environment, and slowly some environmental factors became acceptable. This was an area of learning that Matt decided to tackle in his own time with only gentle encouragement from the sidelines. The hot tub has been a real challenge.

We have had our hot tub for many, many years. He was always asked to join us, and we got used to the same reply of "No thanks" over the years. Then one day, much to our surprise, Matt replied yes. He hunted for his swimsuit and grabbed a towel. As we walked the deck toward the hot tub, I noticed Matt's gait. He was marching—a man on a mission. I could see the determination on his face. He really wanted to tackle this obstacle. Tom took the cover off, and as he did, we could see the trapped steam roll upward. Matt's face changed. He looked worried. I got in knowing he was watching my every move, watching for signs of burning and pain.

"Oh, this feels good," I stated as I sunk into the water. "It's okay, Matt," I coaxed. "Just take it slow." Matt stepped a foot in and simultaneously emitted a hiss. He sat on the side struggling with the idea of submitting another foot to the heat. He had gotten this far before in previous attempts. In each of those attempts, the heat was too much and he had to call it quits, retreating to the house. I waited. If Matt were to come back out, it would show on his face. The look of failure in his eyes was always heartbreaking. This time I could see his face was a mixture of emotion. Yes, I could see fear, but I also saw determination. Matt brought his other foot over the side and into the water. Another hiss as he breathed in. Matt had just gone further than any previous attempt. "If you wait a few seconds, you'll get used to the temperature, and then it will feel good," I said as I moved closer to him. He waited.

Tom coached Matt from behind, I coached Matt from the front, but it was Matt who made the decision to slide in a bit more. He managed to get both thighs in the water. Would he sit? Would he declare he was done? Tom and I watched on, both of us holding our breath. Matt slowly slid into the water and sat on the seat. "It's hot," Matt stated matter-of-factly. Tom got in behind him, making the same hissing sounds and facial expressions Matt had just performed. Tom wasn't trying to mimic Matt—he actually felt the same body shock as Matt. It's interesting to note that Matt glanced at Tom for just a second. Matt's focus was intently on his own body and maintaining his position in the water. I could see he was still forcing himself to stay beneath the surface.

Matt was in. We were in. We all sat for a moment and then asked Matt if he would like us to turn on the water jets. "Yes!" he replied as he nodded his head. Matt was beginning to feel confident. His body was getting used to the water. The expression on his face was more relaxed. We turned on the jets. Matt first experimented with the feel of the current on his hands, and then positioned his body so the water would hit his back. He was actually beginning to enjoy the experience. We talked a while—about little things mostly: the trees, the clouds, the cat coming to join us (walking the perimeter on the rim of the tub). When we got out, Matt hurriedly grabbed his towel and headed for the house. His walk said it all—he was now a master hot tubber!

It's such a slow process to overcome the challenges of autism. Each simple move forward isn't just a happy day for parents; it's a joyous day for the autistic individual too. Don't think for one moment that an autistic person doesn't know when they have beaten one of the challenges. I'm betting Matt keeps a mental list of simple challenges to be met head-on. I can see it on his face, in his body language, and hear it in his speech. A simple thing like getting into a hot tub is not a simple thing to the autistic individual with hypersensitivity to environmental stimuli. Matt had to force himself to feel the pain of hot water. He had to resist the overwhelming urge to pull out. He subjected himself to this environment because not getting in made him different. Matt hates being looked upon as different. So he took up the challenge, faced it head-on, and walked away a champion. How can anyone not admire the fortitude it takes to do what he does almost every day of his life?

JACOB'S WEDDING

OUR FAMILY IS growing. First, Sarah married her fiancé of five years, and then Jacob married his sweetheart the year after. The new members, Paul and Felicia, both treat Matt well, for which I am thankful. It is a wonderful statement to Sarah's and Jacob's character that they each picked spouses that could not only accept Matt for who he is but also put forth effort to understand his world.

This was really brought home to me last fall at Jacob and Felicia's wedding. Wedding planning is a long and arduous task, taking months to prepare, deciding all the details from who will be in the wedding party to the decorations on the tables at the reception. In choosing the groomsman, Jacob had decided to include each one of his good friends and both his stepbrothers, Christopher and Matt, for a total of seven (yes, seven!). He revealed this to Tom and me before he actually asked them, giving me a chance to explain the role of a groomsman to Matt.

Matt hates dressing up—he's a shorts-and-flip-flops kind of guy. I would have to appeal to his love for Jacob if I was going to get a yes out of him. I went in his room and sat down on the edge of his bed. He was playing a video game. I asked him to please pause it. He knew something was up.

"You know Jacob is getting married in the fall, right?" I asked. "Uh, yes," he replied. "In a wedding you have the people that are most important to you stand up with you, and the guys are called the groomsmen," I explained. Matt looked at me funny, as if trying to figure out where all this was leading. "Each grooms-man wears a tux and stands in a long line next to the groom, like in Sarah and Paul's wedding." "Oh yes, I know!" Matt replied. I could tell he was picturing Sarah's wedding the year before and understood the meaning of groomsman.

"Only the special people in Jacob's life are asked to stand next to him," I continued, "and Jacob wants one of those special people to be you." I held my breath, waiting for his comment. If Matt would be uncomfortable or afraid, he would tell me—Matt could be very blunt in his answers. "Oh my" was his only response. I needed to rephrase it a bit. "You are special to Jacob and he wants you to be in his wedding. Will you do this for him?" I held my breath again.

"Yes!" The excitement in his voice was undeniable. I told him Jacob would be asking him soon. When Jacob did ask Matt soon after, Matt gave a smile and a yes, and there were high-fives all around. Matt loves the high-fives. It was a man-type hug, one full of joy and smiles and triumph. Each high-five brought smiles and laughter and great compliments. Months went by without too much discussion about his role until it was time to get the tux fitted. Matt understood the fitting process because he'd had this done for his prom years before. Christopher was also a grooms-man and went with us to get measured. Matt went through the process of fitting the tux as if he had done it a million times before and without complaint.

Next would be the rehearsal. At the rehearsal, Matt met each of the young men involved. As parents of the groom, it was our job to do the rehearsal dinner, and Matt helped us at every turn. He put up tables, put the decorations up, and helped us to turn the activity room at the church into a banquet hall. We would not be having very many items on the menu that Matt would eat, so Tom took Matt on a short road trip to McDonald's for dinner about an hour before the attendants arrived.

Jacob and Felicia had decided we would all eat first and then rehearse. Guests began arriving. Matt sat with Christopher and his date. There were so many people there that Matt had never met, and I worried that he would get uncomfortable and disappear. But Matt stayed in the crowded room, and was engaged conversationally by his brothers and sister and other family members, allowing him to feel part of the group.

During the rehearsal itself, Matt was shown where to stand, where to walk, and what to do. He would be the last of the groomsmen to enter and the last to leave. Felicia had six bridesmaids, leaving Matt to walk to the aisle alone. But a special twist was put into the recessional at this point. Matt would turn at the aisle then stop at the front row and escort me out. We practiced. Matt seemed to take it all very seriously even though the rehearsal was quite playful and joyous. He did enjoy the laid-back atmosphere, but he took his duty to be a very serious affair. Throughout the evening, Jacob and Felicia came by numerous times to talk with him and give high-fives. The bright smile on Matt's face revealed just how much the added attention meant to him.

The next day was the wedding—the big day had finally arrived. Matt put his tux on in the bathroom at the church, Tom handing him each item of clothing. Matt obligingly put them on, a bit overwhelmed by just how much he had to wear and after completing this task followed Tom and Christopher to the room that held the groomsmen and Jacob. Jacob immediately came over and told Matt how good he looked and again gave high-fives. The high-fives kept him focused on Jacob and kept him determined to do his best.

It was hours after dressing before the ceremony actually begun. I kept expecting Matt to just put on the brakes and declare he'd had enough, but that never happened. When the ceremony began, we watched as Jacob entered, followed by each of the grooms-men. Matt was last. He stood at the end of the line and stayed in his position for the entire ceremony. This was very difficult for Matt. He used to just sit down in place or wander off when he was put in this type of position as a young boy. But Matt was not a young boy, he was a man, and his brother was counting on him. You could see the determination on his face—he would not let Jacob down, no way, no how.

When it came time for the recessional, Matt did exactly as he had practiced. His turn at the aisle was a sharp, quick, military-style turn. He took a few steps forward to the first row. As he stopped, he jutted his elbow out in my direction. I proudly took his arm, and we walked back up the aisle to the safety of the vestibule. Matt had done his job exactly as he had been shown with a bit of military flair added in to make it his.

The reception hall was packed. There was room for Tom and me at one of the tables with other family members. Christopher, Sarah, Paul, and Matt were all to sit at the wedding table, but you know how people move around and chairs get pushed from one table to another. An empty chair was available next to Jacob, the chair meant for the best man. The best man had already taken up residence with his own wife at a small table close by. Jacob asked Matt if he would sit with him and Felicia.

Maybe this isn't such a big deal to some, but it was a big deal to me, to Tom, and especially to Matt. Again there were high-fives and smiles all around. Matt was looking very proud. His face said it all. He was sitting with Jacob, and he was honored to do so. Matt took part that day in almost every activity. He even enjoyed it. He never seemed bothered by the crowd of strangers, never looked uncomfortable in his suit—just the shoes (we had him kick those off before entering the reception and replace them with his flip-flops). I never would have imagined that Matt could handle that type of situation, from beginning to end, not in my wildest of dreams. Not only did Jacob and Felicia bond together on that beautiful fall day, but they also cemented their bond with Matt. And for me, well, I was celebrating right along with them and realizing too that I was a witness to another small miracle.

A GLIMPSE OF THE PAST
BRINGS HOPE TO THE FUTURE

I FOUND THE newspaper article on Matt when he was seven. He played T-ball, something autistic children were thought unable to do. Complete with photo. I showed it to Matt. As you know, Matt has no memory of his childhood. He read it aloud, unsure and unsteady, part of him didn't want to know, and part of him had to. As he read it, I wondered if he saw what a miracle he was—he still is.

I went looking for the article because just recently my autism Web site hit 3.5 million, and word got out in my own community, leading to an e-mail requesting an interview from the local newspaper. Instead of feeling excited, Matt was anxious. "No paparazzi" was his only reply. In other words, no cameras please and no questions either. Matt is fine with me talking and writing about him but has no desire to be asked questions about himself and his life. He knows he would be expected to reply, and for him to do that would be stressful. Matt is mostly nonverbal, so I am his voice. He allows me to talk about his life for him, an amazing honor for me.

When I returned home from my interview today, I told him about it and he listened, a stern look on his face. Matt lost his childhood memories in adolescence. When I tell people about him and he is listening, he has that same stern look. He's not sure whether he believes his childhood was like that or not. I can show him pictures, boxes of pictures, but pictures don't show autism. Autism is not a physical handicap, and that makes it almost invisible in photographs. Autism is seen in the behaviors, in social interaction and ability to communicate. It's not readily recognized in the photographs of his smiles while on vacations or at school awards.

"Matt, you have been in the newspaper before, when you were only seven years old." Our eyes met. "Do you remember?" I asked. "No," he replied, his eyes shifting downward. Not being able to remember makes him feel uncomfortable. "Not to worry. I keep everything. Let me see if I can find it." And off I went to dig through files. The first one I came across was of him with his speech therapist. That article was about his therapist, not Matt, but the picture was of the two of them, so I showed it to him anyway.

"Do you remember this one?" That look washed over his face again. He was getting more uncomfortable. He didn't remember. I switched gears. I pulled one of the old newspaper clippings I found of his brother on the high school wrestling team and showed him that one. His face lit up as he recognized his brother's young face. He giggled a bit. Good. He's seeing that it is okay to be in the paper. If his brother was in the news, then it is okay if he was in the news too.

I rummaged around a while longer. Matt had already retreated to his game room when I touched on a yellowed newspaper folded into half twice and wrapped in clear plastic. I removed the wrapper, unfolded the delicate paper slowly and sure enough, there it was. The *Southwest Virginia Enterprise*, May 8, 1993.

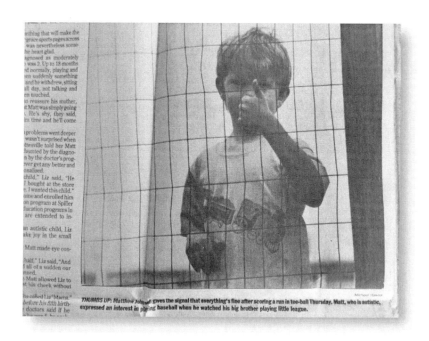

THUMBS UP: Matthew Johnson gives the signal that everything's fine after scoring a run in tee-ball Thursday. Matt, who is autistic, expressed an interest in playing baseball when he watched his big brother playing little league.

Matt was seven years old in 1993, and the only autistic child in his special education classroom. He was the first autistic child in this area to play T-ball. It was almost a full-page article with a huge picture of a very cute little boy standing behind the fence at home plate, giving the photographer a thumbs-up gesture. My memory remembers that day like it was yesterday, but Matt has no memory of it at all.

I laid the paper flat on the counter, smoothed the creases out a bit with my hands, and called for Matt. His walk told me he was unsure. His face told me he was nervous. What would he see? Was he wondering if his autism would show on his face? Would he even recognize that little kid?

He looked at the picture first. There was something in his eyes—a glimmer of recognition maybe? Or was it a relief to not see his autism? Something in his eyes told me he was more curious now than he was afraid. Maybe in examining the face depicted in the yellowed newspaper, he realized the little boy in the photo was actually him. He then read the headline aloud, "Matt Takes His Turn at Bat: Seven-Year-Old Battles His Disability through T-ball." His face scrunched up. He didn't like the title. It had the word *disability*.

"Let's read it, okay?" I nudged. Matt began to read the story aloud. *"Seven-year-old Matt Johnson crossed home plate for the first time Thursday."*

He read on. It talked about his regression, diagnosis, and the hard part, his doctor's prognosis: *"Matt may never get any better and should be institutionalized."*

He read about his first eye contact with me, our first communication through touch (the palm of my hand on his cheek), the first time he called me Mom at age five, and his inability to respond to pain. He stumbled on a few words here and there, but he continued. I could sense he had real interest in his story. His voice was light, almost enthusiastic. Matt was curious, and that filled me with hope. Did Matt remember this?

Did it even matter anymore? After all, he was reading and learning about himself. He was absorbing a bit of his past. Even if he couldn't remember, he could learn about it in a real and tangible way. He was connecting dots to things he knew, things he was told, and he understood. The words discussed his autism, at a time when autism still had a huge role in his day-to-day life, a time when it was rare, a time when nobody had ever heard of the autism spectrum. Matt was learning about himself in a newspaper, and Matt loves to read newspapers.

He also loves baseball, and the news about Matt was also about T-ball. By reading the newspaper, he discovered that before his first T-ball game, we took him out in the yard and practiced going from first base to second base, to third and then home. I remember that day. We bribed him with M&Ms candy, and we thought we had it down until during that first game when he refused to stop at first base after the play officially ended, and insisted he had to go on to home plate. I remember. I remember how wonderfully funny it was. How the umpire about had a stroke when Matt refused to leave the field until he touched all the bases. Some parents yelled in anger, some parents laughed and pointed, but the entire group of neurotypical adults was baffled by the presumed stubbornness of this little boy.

It didn't matter what other parents thought as he tried to touch home plate, we knew why he had to, and we smiled and giggled to ourselves. We understood that we had not taught him all that was needed, and there was the proof, right there, trying to get past the umpire to touch home plate. I remember going to the coach, who went to the umpire. I remember the change on the ump's face when he realized Matt had a handicap. I remember our sense of humor kept us sane. Does Matt?

Matt continued reading aloud, "*Liz hopes one day Matt will be able to live on his own. He is reading on a second grade level now, and she hopes by fourth grade Matt can be taken out of special classes and join a regular classroom.*" He stopped reading and looked at me, directly into my eyes. He's been striving for independence longer than he could remember, quite literally. This year we are hoping to take that huge step. As I watched his body language and facial expressions, I was sure he made the connection. I was pushing for him to be the best he could be even back then. I hoped he understood that I have always had his back. We fight the fight together. That we are, and have always been, a team. Just transitioning to a regular classroom was a massive undertaking, but he did it, and it laid the groundwork for the big dream, his independence, something I've wanted for him just as much as he has wanted it for himself, ever since he was just a little boy. Now Matt knew it too. He understood. His eyes told me so.

"Matt, you went into a regular classroom in the third grade. You changed schools, from Spiller to Sheffey, do you remember? You've always been very smart. I knew you would go into a regular classroom one day," I said. "And you did it a year later."

"Yes, a regular class," he stated confidently. Matt has hated being different, and those few words, "Yes, a regular class," carried an immense amount of meaning. Reading about the plan, knowing it came to pass, knowing he was transitioned to be with other children, which allowed him to graduate high school years later with regular students, held his attention. Was he connecting the dots? I think so. That was such a long time ago—twenty years have passed—and now he was reading about what he was like prior to that big year, when he was still in special education classes. He had always wanted to be a part of a regular class, and in reading the passage, he knew just how far he had come. He knew all that hard work had paid off. I could see his epiphany on his face. No words needed. His expression said it all. Here was proof, in the black and white of the newspaper, that he had made it.

Then Matt read the last paragraph, *"Matt came up to bat in the bottom of the second. On his first swing the bat hit below the ball. Matt's second swing connected for the solid grounder up the middle. He stopped six feet from first base and had to be coaxed to step on the bag. He got tired of staying on second, so he hung out at shortstop for a while. But when the next hit found the outfield grass, Matt rounded third and made it home."*

As he read the play-by-play, the rhythm of his voice got faster. I knew he was excited for this little Matt of long ago. He was rooting for him to make it. He paused at the end of the sentence and turned to look at me. A smile graced his face. That smile was pride. He was very proud that little Matt had rounded the bases and made it home.

Then he looked back at the paper to read the last line. *"They (the doctors) don't give enough hope,"* Liz said. *"You've gotta have hope."*

Again he smiled, turned to look at me, and gave me a big hug. Our eyes met. His were glistening. It hit me hard. I believe Matt understood a little bit more about where he had started and how far he had come. I think he was proud. When he walked back to his game room to play, I noticed he stood a little taller, walked with a bit more confidence.

It was obvious Matt was feeling good about himself. What was he feeling? I can't be sure, but I think it was hope.

LEARNING TO DRIVE

MATT REALLY WANTS his independence. Working toward this goal is a huge undertaking. So far, Matt does his own laundry, cooks his own meals, does pretty good in the area of personal hygiene (but needs work), and keeps his rooms fairly clean. He is able to grocery shop, keep track of his expenses, and is currently attempting e-mail communication. That last one is difficult as Matt is just not much of a communicator—he's autistic.

Yet if Matt is to live an independent life, he must be able to get to where he needs to go, and that means either learning to take a bus, a cab, a subway, or drive himself. We live in a very rural area of Virginia. There are no buses, subways, or cabs. That means Matt needs to learn to drive. When he was a junior in high school, he took driver's education and did real well on the written part of the test. Putting him behind the wheel, however, was not even considered. Matt just was not ready for such a big step.

He's ready now, seven years later. Our first consideration was where to take him. We decided on an old, secluded, and basically abandoned outlet mall to let him practice driving, away from other traffic and distractions. Teaching Matt to drive is not the same as teaching a regular child to drive, but it is similar.

The main difference is how long it takes. Each step is a lesson in patience and practice. For those that have taught their normal children to drive, I salute you. Teaching a child to drive, any child, is scary. Now take that feeling and multiply it to ten and you get close to how it is with an autistic child.

Matt has a routine. He gets behind the wheel and checks his mirrors. He fastens his seatbelt and turns the key. He sits a moment in silence, feeling the hum of the motor and psyching himself up for the practice run. He turns, slowly, deliberately, to look over his shoulder, positioning his right arm to the side and placing his hand on the passenger seat. He puts the car in reverse and backs out of the parking space—at a snail's pace. Once accomplished, a whispered sigh of relief slips out and he faces forward. We sit a few seconds as he mentally prepares to go again. Matt puts the car in drive and applies the gas. We creep along to the end of one small parking lot, and he steps on the brake. My body is jerked forward then back. "Good job, Matt," I say as calmly as I can. "Now let's turn right and go up the hill."

For our first several practices, Matt never got above 5 mph. Then one day as we slowly climbed the hill, I encouraged him to go faster—all the way up to 20 mph. His foot pressed down a little bit, and slowly we climbed to 20 mph. He looks down to watch the speedometer and forgets to watch where he is going. I gently remind him to look at the road. He is startled by the revelation that he forgot to watch where he is going, and I could see a frown start to form. He gets upset with himself for making a mistake, for not being perfect.

Each time we go, Matt practices parking, backing up, driving forward, using his turn signals, and by the end of the session, he is on top of the world. Each time Matt parks the car, he jumps out to admire his newfound skills. If he is between the lines and pleased with himself, his facial expression is one of triumph and he juts his fists into the air as if to say "YES!" If not, the creases in his brow deepen, and he mutters to himself, no doubt scolding himself for not having done better. It's a slow process as he is cautious and nervous and trying desperately to be perfect.

I really hadn't given much thought about his autism other than the slow pace at which we were progressing—that is, not until a bee flew in the window. Matt has always hated flying insects, so much so that he hates going outside for any length of time. He has a real fear of bees. No, Matt has never been stung, but his fear is so intense that one would think so. I was abruptly reminded of this fear when the bee appeared. Matt was slowly driving down one of the parking lanes when out of nowhere a bee flew in his window and immediately flew back out again. In that split second, Matt took both hands off the wheel, covered his face, and unbelievably, kept his foot on the gas. Matt had lost all focus. The car was out of control. "Matt, *break!*" His foot stomped the brake. "Hands on the wheel!" His hands went to wheel. He stopped the car and sat there visibly shaking.

Matt was surprised at what he had done and continued to shake. His mind was racing, and I could see he was angry at himself. Matt hates it when he is not perfect. I could almost hear his thoughts: "Losing control of the car for even a split second is unacceptable…and wrong. How could I make such an awful mistake?" His expression of disgust told me he was berating himself mentally. It took a few minutes of gentle conversation to calm him down.

"Okay, Matt, we know that you will need to keep your windows rolled up," I said. "If you're in traffic and a bug flies in, you have to remain calm, or you'll cause an accident, so to not have that happen, you will need to keep your window up, okay?" That must have sounded reasonable to him as he began to calm down.

We continued to practice before calling it quits for the day. I wanted Matt to end his driving session on a high note, not on the mistake he had made. I waited until he had parked the car perfectly between the lines, jumped out, and thrust his hands in the air in triumph—the sign that he was pleased with himself again. A few days later, when we went on our next practice drive, the first thing Matt did was roll up his window (and simultaneously let out a small "whew").

Teaching Matt to drive is emotionally difficult. I thought I had thought of all the what-ifs. What if he hits a deer, or runs off the road, or has a flat tire, or runs out of gas, or pulled over by a police car or his car breaks down. Unfortunately, I never thought "What if a bug flies in the window?" Still, with all the hurdles we must get over, we have to start somewhere. This is going to take a very long time, possibly years. And as much as it scares me, as much as I want to hold him close and protect him, I know I must let him have his chance to be free and independent.

I keep in mind every day that each driving session, each small lesson learned, is one step closer to the day he becomes independent. I just hope my nerves can stand it.

CHRISTMAS LETTER
TO GRANDMA THELMA

WE ALL HAD such a wonderful time last night at the Christmas dinner at Grandma's house. It was great to have everybody in one place at one time. But this year, well…this year was especially wonderful. I want to thank you, Thelma, from the bottom of my heart.

I want you to know that Matt has always loved going to your house. He is comfortable there. You always have a newspaper for him to read, word-search puzzles for him to concentrate on and something on the television that he enjoys. He loves the news, but he also loves the silly obstacle-course game shows and others that you have going in the background—things I doubt you would watch if not for Matt. There are times when I have wondered if his love of watching the news is an offshoot from time spent in the comfort of your home. I like to think you instilled that in him.

I know Matt can be difficult to buy for—for any occasion—but that has never been a problem for you. You realized so quickly when Matt was young that this kid loves to shop, and the very best gift for him is the money to do so. His expression when he opens the card to find a crisp $50 bill is so joyous—it's apparent that you understand him very well. He is anxious almost immediately, wanting to schedule a whirlwind shopping spree, and on our way home Matt has begun making our plans. The shopping spree is already in the works.

Matt spent the evening comfortably, as if he were right at home, listening to conversations, engaged in the word-search puzzles, or reading the newspaper. He stretched out on your couch to watch a countdown of the "101 Gadgets That Changed the World." He loves history, and he was glued to the TV for the top ten.

Earlier in the evening, his siblings had him laughing so hard he had tears, and the sound of his laughter filled my heart more than I can adequately express. The entire evening was joyous and warm and loving, and I am in awe of the thoughtfulness you showed so effortlessly for my youngest son. This year you really outdid yourself.

The menu even reflected your thoughts of Matt. The menu of our wonderful get-together was so Matt oriented. His favorite vegetables (peas and corn), his favorite food (fries), did not go unnoticed. I am writing to you to express my deepest gratitude for the dinner—it was all so wonderful.

I felt bad that Matt would not eat the chicken tenders. I know you had them for him as his favorite meal is chicken nuggets and fries. But unfortunately, you were not aware there was a difference between nuggets and tenders, and that is my fault, not yours. It is my fault that he didn't eat them because I never made it clear how picky he is about the shape of a chicken nugget. He tried, Thelma, he really did. He took a bite, looked at me with a face filled with worry, and shook his head. He just couldn't eat it. I told him it was okay, that he didn't have to, that you would understand...and you do. Matt was instantly relieved because Matt knew too. He knows how much you love him.

The entire evening was wonderful. I can't remember a better Christmas. It would be a shame if I never told you. You made it all so perfect for everyone. We all had such a great time. But especially, I wanted you to know how much it meant to me and Matt, that it didn't go unnoticed. Matt is difficult to gauge sometimes. It's hard to know what he will eat, what he will do, and what he wants as gifts—but you have really shined these past years in your understanding, compassion, and awareness of his autism. For me, this Christmas was the best Christmas ever for family and loved ones.

That's my own perspective of course. There was so much warmth, laughter, joy, love, and understanding that filled your home that I just couldn't let this experience slip away without saying thank you.

Thank you, Thelma, for being a wonderful mother-in-law and a wonderful grandmother to all of our children. And from the bottom of my heart, thank you for taking the time and expending the energy and demonstrating so much love for my youngest son. It's not easy apparently, since so many people find it so difficult to do so. But you made it seem easy, as simple as breathing.

Thank you. Our Christmas with you was more wonderful than you could have ever imagined.

THE ULTIMATE GOAL

NAVIGATING AUTISM TAKES time, lots and lots of time. It took until Matt was almost five years old for speech to come, and then it was very few words for years after. It took almost seven years to get out of diapers and almost nine to completely be potty trained without the occasional accident. It took until he was almost seven years old to get used to a change in routine, to age twelve to agree to try a new food item, and he was somewhere in his early teens when he started to pick out his own clothes. Autism slows down progress, but the good news is that it doesn't stop progress. Doing something new just takes more time to learn.

I was never in a hurry, except for speech. Speech has a window of opportunity, so we pushed him to speak. Matt saw a speech therapist from his diagnosis at two and a half years old to his day of graduation from high school at nineteen years old. Everything else was mostly accomplished with a bit of steady pressure and a great deal of time. Matt was given equal time to flap his hands and spin his toys and time to focus on learning something new.

Now that "something new" is the move to a place of his very own and a chance at independence. This has also been a long time in achieving. My oldest son, Christopher, bought a house before he moved away. My stepchildren, Jacob and Sarah, both got married before they moved to their own homes. Matt has been a witness to these changes in our family dynamics. He wants his own place too. I call this Matt's "ultimate goal." He has talked about it out loud to himself over the years, and each time he does, his voice is excited and full of energy. He craves it. Living on his own will mean he is in charge, something he needs to make himself feel "normal." Matt has never liked being autistic. To put it bluntly, he hates it. He hates that he is different, that people view him differently. he hates that his speech is not...normal. He hates that he has difficulty understanding communication nuances. He doesn't want people to know. Finding a way for him to accept it as a part of him has been a very difficult task. We are still working on it.

"Autism does not define my son." A nice little phrase I have read a thousand times on blogs and social media pages. Unfortunately, yes, it does. His autism characterizes his speech, his habits, his way of thinking, and yes, it characterizes his daily life. Matt is "more than his autism"—also a nice, popular phrase—and this one is a bit more accurate. Matt is talented (his artwork is astounding), compassionate, friendly, intelligent, and easy to be around. He has a laid-back style that invites interaction. Then his autism makes those interactions difficult and sometimes scary. Social interactions and communication difficulties identify Matt as "different," and Matt hates being different. He wants to blend in, but can't. He wants to hang out, go places, do the things that other people do, and he tries his best to be just another guy, he really does, but he is aware that he is different. Social interactions are very hard. He knows he is different, and it hurts him. If it hurts Matt, it hurts me. Autism is a part of him, the only part of him he dislikes. Moving to an apartment is a wonderful goal, but for Matt it's so much more than just gaining some freedom—it's also a way of trying to shed some of his autism.

Moving out is a complex task for the autistic individual. It's not as simple as packing your bags and going out the door. Moving out is another step toward independence, and because of his autism, it takes time, lots and lots of time. Preparing for independence requires Matt to be able to care for himself. Over the years he has learned to do his own laundry, make his own meals, shop for himself, dress himself, take care of his personal hygiene, feel at ease at the dentist's office, keep track of his finances, use a cell phone, and not freak out when problems arise unexpectedly. He still needs to be able to talk to his doctor, tell someone when he is ill, and seek help when needed, dress appropriately for the weather, be aware of his environment, and foresee consequences of his actions and various situations. We all learn from our mistakes as we navigate our independence. These past several years, Matt has had practice with each of these while in the safety of our home. He has learned much, and continues to do so. Yet I know that most of what he will face alone can only be practiced after the move. It's scary for me, but not for Matt. Matt is ready to take the plunge, and believe it or not, I am ready to let him—scared, but ready. The years have flown by. Where did the time go?

To prepare for this, I had made myself a goal. I set this goal when Matt was between ten to twelve years old. I saw that his autism was dynamic and changing, he was not stuck flapping and spinning, he was not forever echolalic or stuck in a specific routine. Matt was talented, able to learn (graduating number four in his class). He was brave and determined, and he was compassionate. Maybe that doesn't surprise you, but it did me. I was advised to institutionalize my son at age two. I was told he would never be able to do the things he does now. That was in 1988. Parents today know better, but back then, we were fighting against all the odds at a time when autism was only 1:10,000. We were going it alone—there were no other parents to talk to, no specialists to see, no new ideas to research on how to teach, raise a child, or cope with the stresses that came with the diagnosis.

When I realized Matt could do so much more than anyone predicted, I began thinking about the possibility of independence. It took several more years to convince myself that yes, he really could do it. I then set a deadline—something to keep me focused on his progress, nothing more—and that deadline was before Matt turned thirty years old. This was a huge step, just to consider the possibility. It also seemed far enough away to prepare him for the challenge and long enough for me to get used to the idea. Matt will soon be twenty-seven years old, and the "ultimate goal" deadline is looming closer. For the first time since his diagnosis, I actually believe all the way to my soul that he can do this. Matt made me believe.

Next summer I will be looking at apartments, researching adult disability services and transportation options. No group homes are on the table. First, the closest adult autism services are several hundred miles from here, not an option. Second, Matt does not want to be with other disabled adults because he is trying to get as far away as possible from any reminder of his own disability. He would never allow it. Matt needs an apartment, close to shopping, and he needs transportation. He may need a social worker to oversee his health care and living arrangements, but most importantly, he needs me to understand his need to be as independent as possible. It will be a slow transition. He will have either my husband or me staying with him four to five nights a week at first. Then we will cut down on the number of overnight visits to three, then two, then one. It will take time, lots and lots of time. Taking our time to work on each aspect of his autism has worked pretty well thus far. We are in no hurry. We want him to be as comfortable as possible and transition into the realm of independence slowly, flattening out those bumps in the road as we find them. I am very proud of my son for the determination and courage he displays as we move toward the ultimate goal.

Recently, Matt said to me in a very serious and determined voice, "I will have my own place. I can do this!" He wasn't just affirming to himself that it was possible. He had directed the comment at me. Matt was assuring me it was possible. I believe him. Only time will tell if Matt can really handle independence, but I know that if we take it slow and easy, the chance of success is pretty darn good. It's time for me to start letting go. It's amazing to just picture Matt in his own place, knowing what he had to overcome to get to this point. It's true. Nothing is impossible. Navigating autism just takes time.

THE WHISPERED SECRET

PART I

EVER HAVE A secret that even though you were glowing inside, you just couldn't tell anyone? There are all kinds of secrets: the kind that you carry as a burden, the kind that brings tears, the kind that fills your heart. What if you couldn't tell anyone, not because you wanted to keep the secret, but because you seriously couldn't tell? You just couldn't find the words? What if that part of your brain still struggled to connect thoughts to words? In other words, the thoughts-to-words neural highway was still under construction?

I was reminded of this yesterday. My son Matt is autistic and mostly nonverbal. He speaks about three to four good sentences a day, a huge increase from his mostly silent childhood. Yesterday we were on our way to town to see a movie. Matt was in a really good mood, excited to be going to the movies, shopping, and out for pizza. As usual, I prompted him to speak by asking simple questions. It was just him and me in our Jeep, traveling on the interstate toward town. It was one of those mother-and-son kind of days. I noticed Matt grinning. I smiled in return.

"What are you thinking about, Matt?" Now I expected him to say something about the movie we would see that evening or maybe something about what he was planning to buy, or maybe his mind was on the fact that his daddy would be coming home late tonight from his job in a neighboring state. I expected Matt to say one of those things in his matter-of-fact way of conversing. But none of those things were on his mind.

"I was thinking about last fall, in Radford. I saw a semi-truck," he began as he leaned in close and half covered his mouth as if to tell me a wonderful secret. This was unusual behavior, and I instinctively leaned in toward him in return.

When he could almost reach my ear, he whispered excitedly, "It was a Books-a-Million truck in the southbound lane headed to Bristol!"

Wow. I wasn't prepared for that. I immediately went into decipher mode. I know Matt loves books. He loves to read, and he loves bookstores where every kind of book imaginable surrounds him. But what took me back a bit was the way in which he told me. This was a huge secret he had been unable to share with anyone. He must have thought about it ever since he had seen that truck months ago. He must have thought about how it had been headed south (using the signs on the interstate, or maybe the address was on the truck) and wondered about where that store might be in Bristol.

"It was? Really?" I replied. "Yes, and remember at ETSU?" he continued. That remark meant he had seen another store close to the campus of Eastern Tennessee State University in Johnson City, Tennessee. Many years ago, we had visited his stepsister there at school. Did he see the bookstore way back then and been longing to go ever since? He doesn't use the Internet, so I know all of this information had to be from the sign on the truck or from road signs, or even memories of trips taken years ago when he was a young boy. I did a search on the Internet last night, and sure enough there's a store listed in each city.

I thought about his desire to go in search of this massive book-store—an adventure so desirable, so magnificent, that he couldn't even find the words to tell me until now. I thought about how he must have been dreaming about it for at least the past four to six months, maybe for years, before excitedly whispering it in my ear.

Maybe you are wondering what the big deal is. If you are the parent of a mostly nonverbal autistic child, I am sure you understand. You understand how precious this moment was. He leaned in and *whispered* it to me! It meant something very special to him, and until that particular moment in time, Matt had not been able to voice it to anyone. He simply couldn't find the words to tell me. Although the desire must have been great, Matt had not been able to ask me to take him there. He couldn't tell me, not until yesterday. Not until everything came together in a specific moment in time—driving on the interstate, alone with his best friend (his moniker for me) who could take in all his forms of communication and understand both his words and his joy. But more importantly, his neural highway, which connects thoughts to words, was clear from obstruction.

I gave Matt a big smile and gave him what he needed me to say, "How about we go in search of the store this summer? We'll take a day and drive to Bristol. Sound good?" I asked. "Yes!" he replied and pumped his fist into the air above his head. Mission accomplished. The energy of his joy completely filled the air around us.

I have always been very observant of my son, and over the years, I have become quite good at deciphering all of Matt's com-munication forms. Communication goes both ways. I teach him how to converse verbally and he teaches me how to converse silently. Our conversations usually contain few words, and yet we communicate very well. This deeper form of interaction has allowed me to address that which scares him, that which bothers him, and that which makes him happy. But yesterday was a first. His excitement was so powerful that he had to whisper it to me.

I knew I had just witnessed something I had not seen in Matt's twenty-seven years—the precise moment in time when his joy and his words had finally made it past the roadblock on his thoughts-to-words neural highway. Not only did he pass that roadblock, he sped past it so quickly that his words sprang forth and just bubbled out of him in the most powerful way. The long-held secret had been released...finally.

I was so touched by the moment that I had to fight back the tears as my heart soared. It touched me in a way that is difficult for me to explain (and I have no language roadblocks). All I can tell you is that the whispered secret of his heartfelt desire was more powerful in its delivery than shouting it from the rooftops ever could be. It was a whisper. A restrained but excited voice that had found a way through the roadblock where nothing else could, and I was there in that moment to hear it slip past.

I learn something new about my son every day, even twenty-five years after the diagnosis of autism. A small step forward... every...single...day. The sun is just now coming up, and I am wondering, "What wondrous thing shall I witness today?" Of course, I won't know until it happens. And although right now this new day has not revealed its secrets, I do know that some secrets, especially whispered ones, are definitely worth waiting for.

PART II

Today was the big day, the day we would go in search of the Books-A-Million (BAM) store in Bristol. Matt had expressed his immense desire to find this particular store in an excited whisper that told me just in the sheer expressiveness of his body language that this specific store held something immensely powerful for him. Today was the day the wish, the desire, and the longing would all be fulfilled. Today his secret would see the light of day.

Matt had gone to bed early last night, a very difficult change to his night-owl routine. He knew we would be leaving at 9:00 a.m., and therefore going to bed at his usual time (7:00 a.m.)

was not a good idea. We made a plan. He would get up early the day before so he could be tired enough to go to bed early later that night. I hoped he would get at least a few hours' sleep. Amazingly, Matt willingly changed his own routine and was in bed early (12:00 midnight), a whole seven hours earlier than normal. Unfortunately his excitement hindered his wish for sleep, and he only managed a few hours before rising at 7:00 a.m. That's when he jumped out of bed, got dressed, put his hat on, put his wallet and camera in his pockets, and grabbed one of his favorite Van Halen CDs for the travel music.

I caught him coming down the hallway and reminded him to brush his teeth.

He set his CD down and headed straight toward the bathroom, mumbling, "Okay, one last thing before we hit the road." His desired trip just minutes from becoming a reality had ramped up his outer monologue. It was continuous. The "outer monologue" is what I call Matt speaking his thoughts to himself out loud, something he has done most of his verbal life. When he is excited, the words pour forth, in private and to himself. How I wish he could speak to me as well as he can to himself!

Although I wish for more, I am grateful for what I do have. I know so much about my son simply because I have learned to listen to his outer monologues discreetly from another room. They have given me insight into areas of my child's thoughts I would not otherwise know of. This morning, his outer monologue continued even with the toothbrush humming and with a mouth full of foam, a sign that his excitement could not be contained even for a few minutes. I wish I knew what he had said, but the foam impeded the clarity of his voice, and I was left not knowing the gist of the conversation, only that he said it excitedly.

Finally, everyone was ready, and we headed out the door and toward Tom's car. Matt was so light on his feet he was floating, the smile on his face stretching from ear to ear. That beautiful smile never dimmed during the entire one-and-half-hour trip to

Bristol. In addition, he sang with his favorite Van Halen songs, laughed, and excitedly counted the mile markers on the interstate. The closer we got, the more excited his voice. He spotted our exit and immediately sat up straighter and stared out the window as if he were trying to force the BAM store to come into view by sheer willpower. There it was! Hurray!

And then as we pulled into that magical parking lot, I heard him exclaim, "Dream come true since coming home on my birthday from Montgomery, Alabama!"

What? That was January of 2011! OMG! Has Matt been thinking of this trip for over two years? I was astonished. "Matt, do you mean you have wanted to come here since 2011?" I asked. "Yes!" he replied.

He popped out of the car as soon as it stopped, leaving me to wonder why he could not tell me sooner. What magical draw did this particular store have on my son? Matt headed for the door. He paused, knowing we wanted a picture first, turned, and smiled for the camera, then hurriedly entered the store. He took only a few seconds to get his bearings and then proceeded down the aisle like a man on a mission. Not wanting to hover, Tom and I went to get coffee. With hot coffee in hand, we leisurely strode in the direction Matt was last seen taking and found him in the comic-book section.

Upon seeing us, he exclaimed, "Mission accomplished!" and held out his arms. In each hand was a book. I recognized the cover art for each immediately. His favorite animation characters graced their covers—*Rurouni Kenshin* (manga series, volumes 8 and 9). That is when we finally learned the story behind the desire of the whispered secret.

Matt talked a mile a minute, leaving words out, mispronouncing a few more in his rush to release the long-awaited information, and this is what I learned:

1. The BAM store closest to us in Blacksburg closed in 2011. Matt had read about the closing in a newspaper at his grandma's house that same year.

2. On the way back from Montgomery, Alabama, where he had been on an adventure with Tom (Tom's work assignment was for thirteen weeks, and Matt had gone for the last four weeks), Matt had seen the sign for BAM at the Bristol exit number 1.

3. Matt's favorite store was Barnes and Noble, where he bought his favorite animation books, volumes 1 to 7. They did not have volumes 8 or 9, the last two in the sequence. Each time we had gone, he searched for them. He realized

that he would not be able to complete the set by shopping at Barnes and Noble.

4. Last summer Matt had seen a BAM tractor-trailer headed for Bristol. He knew his best chance to complete the set was to go to BAM. He remembered there was one in Bristol, exit number 1.

5. Wanting to go but unable to convey the information to me, Matt was stuck with a desire and a need and no way to fix the problem. His communication deficit—bringing up a topic, asking a question, saying what was on his mind—all prevented him from conveying these things to me. Matt held a secret because he had no choice.

6. A few months ago, his thoughts-to-words neural highway unblocked long enough to allow a glimpse of his desire to come rushing out in a whispered secret to me on our way to town.

There's more. I learned something too. I learned that Matt can push himself to tell me something he needs me to know, that it isn't impossible. I heard an entire explanation today. I pieced together his statements, reiterated them back to Matt, and asked if they were correct. He corrected a few points I had gotten backward and when I had it correct, he smiled real big and said, "Yes!" like I was his favorite pupil ever!

With our mission accomplished, we headed out toward more shopping and lunch, and I thought about what I had learned today. I turned and looked at Matt. "You will need to do this more often when you live on your own, Matt. You will need to say, 'Mama, I want to go to the store, I want to go shopping. I need to get something,' so you will need to keep practicing this."

Matt took only a second to digest this information then looked at me and said, "Mama, I need to go shopping."

"Excellent practice, Matt!" I replied.

Matt's face beamed with pride.

He will practice—we will practice. The words will come. It will get easier—for both of us. I won't need to wonder constantly, and he won't need to hold it all in. It's a great goal, a goal that I had thought so much about over the years. We have such a unique way of communicating, using body language, facial expressions, behaviors and nuances, and it has worked well, but I have known all along he needs more. Our communication had gotten to be so ingrained that I had to force myself to start asking him questions I already knew the answer to just to get him to practice speaking. Now I realize that this strategy has worked. This wonderful young man has thoughts he would like to share if he could just find the right road on the thoughts-to-words neural highway. He has roadblocks and obstacles on that road that still need clearing away—but it is something we can do together, slowly, and we can improve as we continue to practice.

It's scary being a mom of an autistic child because I know it's all on me to be the best teacher and mentor I can possibly be to this wonderful son of mine. Today I was blessed to witness the result of all those years of prodding him to speak, to answer questions, and to share himself with me as best he can, and I feel victorious!

All those days of asking the same questions: "What are you thinking about, Matt?" "We're going shopping today, Matt, what do you need?" The kinds of questions that forced him to complete a sentence, express an emotion, and think about the immediate future. I must have asked those two particular questions thousands upon thousands of times over the years. I realized today, just this minute, that it was all that practice that allowed Matt to whisper his secret to me months ago, and to explain to me today *why* he needed to go, *what* he was looking for, and *how long* he had been thinking about it.

So maybe, just maybe, there will come a day when my son will not be "mostly nonverbal." Maybe, just maybe, all that practice will pay off like the lottery—speaking on a daily basis and with me watching his communication get easier. But for today I feel tremendously blessed as I shared in his joy, learned the mystery behind the whispered secret, and found myself hopeful for a future where the words will come exactly when he needs them to.

HOW A SIMPLE RAINY DAY PUSHED
THE LIMITS OF ENDURANCE

IT WAS A day to remember—the annual home game at Virginia Tech. It was a close battle on the field, and an even bigger battle in the stands as my severe-to-moderate autistic son pushed the envelope of his own endurance. I watched as he fought against the sensory stimulation induced by the feel of rain, and I watched helplessly as the stimulation tripped his overload switch. For many autistic people, too much sensory stimulation can overload their ability to process—things such as loud noises, strong smells, bright lights, and certain textures are just too much to bear. Sometimes, a parent can intervene and help them fight (by providing headphones, sunglasses, and gloves), and on occasion, when all else fails, we simply need to remove them from the stimulus altogether.

On game day this year, I watched as Matt fought an epic personal battle against the onslaught of environmental stimulation of epic proportions. His personal endurance was forced right up to the edge of the cliff, and only his determination to endure kept him from going over that edge. It was a day that again reminded me just how much autism affects his everyday life and even simple pleasures.

Matt is twenty-seven years old and has loved Virginia Tech for at least twenty of those years. He decorates his rooms in maroon and orange, wears a VT T-shirt, VT sandals, and a VT hat almost daily, and even has a VT couch (orange and maroon with the VT emblem) in his game room. My husband and I take him to one home game every year, and Matt's excitement about the upcoming event permeates our home for months prior. For the big event this year, he requested the tickets for the battle against Marshall in late September. Matt has over thirty different T-shirts with Virginia Tech or Hokies emblem on them, but for the epic battle this year, he had to purchase another one—to wear only on game day. For over a month, he marked an X through each day on his calendar leading up to his big day and made sure to remind me just how many more days we had to wait. A week before the scheduled day, the forecast predicted rain for game day—it was my "heads-up" to be prepared.

Game day arrived along with ominous gray clouds overhead. We were not deterred from our mission though and proceeded to dress in the home-team colors, grabbed our rain gear, and headed out the door. A few misting drops started to fall. It looked like the weather prediction may be correct, a chance of intermittent storms all day. I focused on the "intermittent" part.

We parked in our usual spot—a good distance from the stadium but one in which the walk took us past all the revered sights across campus. This was our routine each year, and we couldn't deviate from the routine, not without good cause. A few sprinkles of rain were not considered "good cause." As expected, Matt began snapping picture after picture as soon as his feet hit the pavement. He loved taking pictures of his favorite buildings and pathways, which marked the beauty of the Virginia Tech campus, his visual record of his favorite place in the whole world. The mist morphed to drizzle, and we walked on.

Matt wore a VT jacket with a hood as protection against the rain that fell, but his hood stayed down—his beloved VT hat protected his head. I had made sure that morning that he was covered head to ankle (his toes were exposed due to his insistence on wearing his VT sandals) and was fairly confident he was well covered and protected against the elements, but just in case, we brought along our rain gear (plastic capes). Unfortunately, Matt hates wearing the rain capes, he hates the feel of plastic on his skin, and umbrellas are not allowed in the stadium. His jacket would have to do. At first, the light rain didn't seem to bother him as he kept to his usual routine of snapping pictures while we walked across the campus, but as we neared the halfway point, the rain started to come a bit faster, and in response, Matt put away his camera and quickened his pace.

Once inside the stadium, we shook off the dampness of our coats and purposefully took our time getting to our seats, staying under the overhang as long as possible before returning to the open air and the elements. A small break in the clouds would have felt like heaven by then, but instead as we walked up the stadium stairs toward our seats, the sky grew darker and the rain continued to fall. We laid a sweatshirt over the wet cement bench and sat down. I glanced at Matt. He seemed oblivious to the rain and instead seemed focused on where he was and the game before him. His smile had not been dimmed by the dampness I knew he felt. As I looked at my son, I thought, "Good. You can do this, Matt, I just know you can."

The game began…and the rain fell harder.

I put on my rain gear, Tom put on his rain gear, and Matt pulled his hood over his hat. I asked him to zip his jacket, and he did so hurriedly, not because he was getting wet but because he wanted to keep his eyes on the field as he might miss something important, like what the Hokie Bird mascot was up to. Each quarter came and went, and the rain continued. Minute after minute, hour after hour, it just kept raining. It fell hard at times and less at others, but the rain never let up. The game was neck and neck, and Matt's focus seemed to be on the field, the players, the score, and keeping track of where the Hokie Bird was at all times. That was during the first half. As for the weather, he appeared to be handling the rain fairly well.

It wasn't until the halftime break when I noticed the cracks in his armor. When we were under the shelter and out of the rain, Matt suddenly shook his hands violently in an "I can't stand it!" motion. Tom and I instinctively handed him some paper towels, which he took gratefully, and immediately used them to cover and wipe his hands over and over, as if he couldn't dry his hands fast enough. His spirits were still high, but not as high as they had been. The feeling of being wet and damp was starting to crack his armor of determination. It was starting to get to him.

We stood under the shelter of the breezeway and ate our lunch, hot dogs that were too overcooked and way too overpriced. Matt had looked forward to it all morning, but now he seemed distant. He ate his hot dog, but there was no enthusiasm in it, not like in previous years. These were stadium hot dogs and therefore a special Hokie treat for him, but he ate it like it was a chore. I knew he was uncomfortable, pushing his limits, and we delayed going back to our seats as long as we could. "You ready to go back, Matt?" I asked. "Yes," he replied, not excited, not happy, just resigned to go back to the uncomfortable exposure to the elements, something which must be endured in order to watch his favorite team play from the seats in his favorite stadium. So back we went for the second half...and an even harder rain.

We endured by focusing on the play-by-play on the field, by cheering, grunting at fumbles, and chanting the H-O-K-I-E at each touchdown. The opposing team was a force to be reckoned with, and the atmosphere stayed tense and exciting—the perfect football game. Unfortunately, it was not the perfect weather. Although my son appeared to be fully engaged in the events on the field, I knew that deep down he was really fighting against the feel of the rain and fighting the urge to leave. After hours and hours of continual rain, I knew his limits were being pushed. The rain had by now seeped down onto his shirt, soaked his jeans, and was steadily dripping off his hood onto his face. His feet must have been ice cold, and through it all he appeared outwardly to be fine. In reality he was overloading and fighting to remain calm. The game was almost over—he watched the clock...could he make it? Then in an upset, the score tied and the game went into overtime.

Matt had set a limit, had forced himself to stay until the clock ran out on the fourth quarter, and when the game went into overtime, you could see he had not planned for that. He had taken all he could, almost five hours of it, and he just couldn't take anymore. Enough was enough.

"I need to go now," he said urgently to Tom. Tom looked at me in shock and whispered, "Matt said he needs to go!" "Okay, then we go," I replied and started to grab my things. "But we're tied and in overtime!" Tom said, bewildered. "Yep, but if Matt said he needs to go now, then he must *really* need to go," I said, looking into Tom's eyes and giving him the "think about it" look. It clicked. I saw it on Tom's face.

Tom understood we were on the brink of an emergency situation. Matt's body was going into overload—too much rain, too much wet, too much cold. His body just couldn't do it any longer. We had to leave—right now! As we stood to leave, the sky darkened even more, and the real storm moved in. It poured buckets, drenching us in seconds. Rain—hard, cold streams of rain now assaulted my son, and there was absolutely nothing I could do to stop it. Tom took off his rain cape in an attempt to protect Matt from the downpour, but Matt, on the edge of overload, could not accept it. For Matt, wearing rain gear would just add insult to injury, and he politely refused. I took off my sweatshirt from underneath my rain cape and gave it to Matt to use as a makeshift umbrella, which he gladly took and put over his head. As we walked, we heard the play-by-play of the game continue. VT was in their second overtime.

It was a very, very long walk back to the car. Every step was purposeful and not quite fast enough. Up a hill, down a flight of stairs, round a bend, and down another flight of stairs—the path back seemed never ending, and the rain came down even harder. By the time we got to the car, we were thoroughly drenched. Matt had been quiet the whole way—never said a word, never took a picture, and never smiled. It was all he could do to just keep moving. My son was withdrawing, shades of his earlier years of autism and a protective measure when things got to be too much. This was one of those times. I recognized it immediately even though he had not resorted to this behavior in over fifteen years. Once we were inside the vehicle, Tom turned on the heat and the radio. The announcer was overjoyed, exclaiming VT had won in their third overtime! Matt smiled. "Yes!" he said softly. His favorite team had won, and although he was physically miserable, he was happy. His withdrawal ended.

I tried to keep him engaged while we rode home, trying my best to keep his mind on something, anything other than the cold and wet that enveloped his body. An hour later, we were home and got out of the car, walking in the rain one last time as we headed for the door. Matt went straight in, changed his clothes, and lay down on his couch, covering himself with a blanket. Minutes later he was asleep. He had done all he could do, and it had worn him out, both physically and mentally. Mother Nature had thrown all the rain it could at him, and he had endured.

This was a story of endurance, of a young man with autism who set his mind to take whatever the weather handed out, pushing the limits of his own stamina. Every atom of his being must have been screaming at him to leave. This was his much-loved yearly game, one that went into three overtimes and was truly a fingernail-biting showdown between equally matched titans. For Matt to have to leave before the end meant he had hit the wall. He did what he could and left when enough was enough. But don't focus on the fact that he had to go before it was over. No, that would be missing the point entirely. Focus instead on the amount of time he stayed, over four hours of unrelenting rain, and the amount of difficulty he must have endured. Over four hours of rain, rain, and harder rain… Four hours! He met it head on with determination and quiet resolve and inner strength.

The experience of that day highlights the reality of sensory-processing difficulties and shows just how far my son has come over the years, because you see, Matt never outgrew tactile sensitivity. He's battled it all his life. It's in knowing this that begs the question, "How was he able to make it that long under those conditions?" Matt has learned over the years to push himself in all things, to endure and not let the uncomfortable stimuli take control his body or his life. It's not something I taught him. It's something he has always had within him. Pushing the envelope—that's who he is, that's how he endures, and that's how he manages to still have a life with simple pleasures regardless of the obstacles autism throws his way.

I know my son is not alone. Many autistic people fight against the environment every day, and no one sees, no one knows, because on the outside they appear calm. They have learned how to endure the assaults on their senses that occur daily, something we can't even imagine, and most, like my son, do it with dignity and quiet grace.

It's experiences like these that always strike the heart of my very being. Matt has endured more in his short life on a daily basis than most people will ever have to deal with in their entire lives, and that makes him the bravest soul I will ever know.

COMPARING AUTISTIC
APPLES AND ORANGES

THIS PAST WEEK I spoke to a woman who has an autistic son. Her son goes to Virginia Tech and is majoring in history. He loves reading and writing papers and is doing very well.

Of course he is. After all, college is all about reading and writing papers. His memory is exceptional, and exams are a breeze for him. He is on the honor roll consistently. I listened as she told me all these things and found myself excited for her.

Yet underneath my excitement, I felt something else too. I felt myself getting anxious. My heart even raced a bit. I felt a few pangs of sadness. It haunted me to the point where I wanted to put our conversation out of my mind. Unfortunately, I found it to be quite impossible to forget. Instead, I ended up thinking about her son all weekend and wishing terribly that my son was engaged in college activity. Don't get me wrong, I was truly happy for her and her son. But to be honest, I couldn't help but wish Matt was at Tech, learning, exploring, and making new friends. I hate to admit it, but I think my sadness was intricately tied to another emotion, envy.

Matt wants so badly to go to Virginia Tech. He wants to be a part of the college crowd and take in the feel of the campus and campus life. Unfortunately, Matt hates to write papers, and he absolutely hates being tested—on anything. To be at VT he would need a facilitator, a very good one. Someone who could focus him and make him feel comfortable during exams. They would need to have a great deal of patience and provide him with alternative explanations for each lecture. Matt's ability to both socialize and learn is very fragile. If I could be his facilitator, I would. But it isn't as simple as that. Matt needs more time to become his own person. This means he cannot fulfill his dreams, at least not yet. This is what makes me sad, and yes, a bit envious.

ASD (autism spectrum disorder) means that his autism lies somewhere on the vast spectrum between mild and severe. It means that his skills are not the same as other autistic individuals, nor are his weaknesses. Matt is unique in his combination. Each individual on the spectrum is also unique—in their behaviors, their skills, their personalities, and their weaknesses. This also means that each of us who cares for someone with autism deals with different challenges and different circumstances. What we all have in common is our desire that our specific child will excel in their life activities and continually overcome the hurdles placed before them, especially those difficulties associated with autism.

Who has not heard of Temple Grandin? Don't we all want our autistic children to shine in similar fashion to Ms. Grandin? Don't we all want them to go above and beyond the suspected limitations that were presented to us so coldly by the medical professionals upon diagnosis? I don't know how everyone else feels, only how I feel. I don't know what everyone else can do for their child, only what I can do for mine. I can't push Matt too hard, and I can't give up on him either. I know his capabilities, but I also know his weaknesses. I've seen what happens if I push too hard or push him in a direction he is unprepared for. He regresses. He burrows inward away from the stress. This is how

Matt copes. I can't bear to watch him regress, and so I take it slow, very slow.

And then I hear about a young man Matt's age and how well he is doing in college, and I wonder if I have done something wrong. Have I gone too slowly with Matt? Have I really kept his best interests at heart? Where would Matt be now if I were a better mother, a better teacher, a better advocate?

I am happy for that mother and her family and proud of her son at Virginia Tech. I am also a bit envious—of her, her child, Temple Grandin, and other high-functioning, high-achieving autistic individuals. Not because they are any better than my son Matt. No. No. I've done a lot of soul-searching this weekend and have found my sadness and my envy actually stem from her confidence. She seemed so sure of her son's future. She knows her son will be fine on his own one day because he can handle college life and college-level stress. I, however, am not certain of my own son's future. What will happen down the road? Will he live on his own? Will he be able to handle the stress of life without me as his shield? These are the things I fear and struggle with each day. It isn't how far one goes in their education, but how well one can deal with everyday stress.

In the final analysis, I find it isn't so much envy as it is simple fear. Hearing about the success of another gives me hope (as well it should), but it also reminds me of how far we have yet to go to secure Matt's future. Matt is not high functioning. He is moderate/severe and mostly nonverbal. He is autistic and he is unique. His goals are specific for him. His achievements are his own. What will his life be like later as an adult? What do I really, truly want for my son? When it comes right down to it, the most important thing I want for my son is for him to be happy, just happy.

Matt isn't in college right now. He isn't dealing with deadlines, exams, peer pressure, or reading assignments. He doesn't use an alarm clock or punch a time clock. Presently, Matt is happy. He likes who he is. He likes his life, loves his family, and is eager to keep learning new skills. That's all I have really ever hoped for. Upon realizing that simple truth, I finally found my own peace. So comparing a high-functioning autistic to a moderate/severe autistic child, or a verbal child to a nonverbal child, is like comparing autistic apples and oranges. Instead, look at what your child can do, what they are capable of, and push in your own way. Don't use the skills of others as a measuring stick for your own child. It's called a spectrum for a reason.

Matt is happy, and that means I have exactly what I wanted.

A PARTY IS NOT JUST A PARTY— IT'S SOCIAL INTERACTION TO THE EXTREME!

I AM ALWAYS amazed at the continued learning that takes place for my son, long after high school and deep into his adult life. A diagnosis of autism brings with it so many misconceptions, one of which is that the behaviors witnessed in a two-and-a-half-year-old are permanent. Of course they are not, as many parents will attest to. They are ever changing throughout their early years, regardless of which therapy is chosen. As long as there are loving interactions and a willingness to accept that autism requires a different way of learning and, for parents, a different way of teaching, then anything is possible.

Over the twenty-seven years of navigating the ups and downs of autism, I know my son, Matt, is learning in his own way how to communicate and interact socially. There are times when my role has been simply as his cruise director, helping him enjoy an experience in which I know is difficult for him to participate in. Never had this been clearer to me than this week as Matt and

I attended a party for my mentor, Fred, who was retiring from teaching college science.

Fred was one of my science teachers when I returned to college to seek a degree in biology. He offered research experience as one of his course selections, research on spiders, and I was eager to learn and get that experience. The research required me to come in at odd times and even weekends, and with no babysitter, I decided to make these trips an adventure for our four children. I remember their first time in the spider lab. They were all so curious and eager, all except for Matt. Matt was curious too, but scared. He remained in the hallway just outside the door, pacing back and forth as he listened to the questions and answers from a safe distance.

It took several trips before Matt could bring himself to enter that creepy room with spiders in boxes, fruit flies in vials, strange musty smells, humming computers, and bright lights. He finally went in, and he eventually began to feel safe enough to look at the tall, bearded stranger that hung out there on occasion. Fred always laughed and smiled, the key to encouraging Matt to accept him as one of the good guys.

Matt rarely spoke a word in those years, so communication was mostly through Fred's humor and my translation to Matt in short, precise sentences and then describing everything to him in detail when we would return home. Matt learned about spiders, about research, and came to like the gentle giant known as Fred.

I returned to the same college again for my master's degree, and I would take Matt along on occasion for more adventures. Matt was older and very willing to walk with my husband around campus, taking pictures and exploring all the new areas while I was in class. He had become intrigued with college campuses, and one of his favorites was Radford, also my favorite, and the place where he saw Fred. While on campus, Matt would have to stop by the library, another favorite place, so he could check out the science books and magazines. Science had become his favorite subject. We also would swing by Fred's office to see if he was there and just to say hello.

Years later, I returned to the same campus as an adjunct science instructor. Matt was thrilled with the news and eager to explore once again the campus of so many good childhood experiences. The campus was still growing. There was always something new to see.

How many times did he run into Fred over all those years? There were numerous occasions for a friendly "hello" and "what have you been up to lately?" Each chance encounter renewed his memory of his favorite gentle giant.

Last week I received the e-mail invitation to Fred's retirement. I excitedly told Matt of the event, and without missing a beat, he wrote it on our calendar in big bold letters. He didn't have to think about it, didn't wonder if he could manage to be around so many strangers, didn't ask what it would be like, or become anxious (like he does when I invite him to picnics and other events). Not this time. This time Matt just took it as common knowledge that he was going with me.

There would be almost one hundred people attending. Matt would know only one. Could he really do this? Up to now, Matt had never wanted to go to parties. He didn't like picnics or large events unless family was involved and always expressed a simple no when asked if he wanted to attend. Just *wanting* to go to Fred's retirement party was therefore a new milestone, another barrier broken through. The big questions in my mind were "How would he react?" "Would he be able to handle the sounds of voices, the movements of strangers, and the smell of foods he would never attempt to even taste?"

I've been navigating autism for a very long time now, so it was just natural to take care of the small roadblocks to his enjoyment of the evening. I basically paved the way for a smooth night. The first thing we did was drive to the location of the party the day before. It was to be at a retreat in the woods. We drove the long, winding path so Matt could memorize the signs and the land-scape. He even took a few pictures of the mountain views.

The next day I made sure we stopped for his favorite meal of chicken nuggets on the drive there. I purposefully arrived an hour late until I knew most people were already there, so Matt could ease into the room without wondering what to do. All the attention would be on Fred. The speeches were under way when we entered, and Matt immediately picked out Fred. His joy at seeing his favorite spider man was obvious. A smile graced his face from ear to ear.

When the speeches were over, we made our way to Fred, who greeted us enthusiastically and spoke to Matt as naturally and lighthearted as always. Matt took pictures and even gave me his camera so I could take one of him with Fred.

I saw other people I wanted to speak to also, some I had not seen in ages, and Matt followed along. As soon as he glanced downward and paced back and forth, a sign of distress, I knew that was my cue to introduce him and brag on his preparations for the big move to his own place. The person listening took that cue from me and ran with it, asking Matt simple questions that allowed him to focus on his plans and his joy.

One conversation I was having soon became unexpectedly extended, and when I looked up, I noticed that Matt had walked away. I scanned the room once or twice and finally decided to search for him. I found him in the hallway reading the posters, something he likes to do at the college. He really didn't want to go back in, but he didn't want to leave.

I was expecting this dilemma and asked him if he needed a drink. I had brought a cooler of soft drinks and left them in my Jeep for just such an excuse to casually get out and away from the commotion for a few minutes. He jumped at the chance, thank-ful he had a reason to take a break. Appearances, after all, are everything to Matt.

We took our time and slowly walked in the dark toward the Jeep, commenting on the stars and the beautifully warm evening. Once there we sat for a few minutes, and I asked him a few questions and made small talk until I could gauge how he was faring. After a few minutes of downtime, I could see he was ready to go back in for round 2.

People were beginning to leave by then, and the crowd was thinning out. That helped Matt feel more at ease. We once again got a chance to actually speak with Fred a bit more, and Matt's smile was bigger than ever. I introduced Matt to Fred's wife, Cindy, who was just as warm and gentle as her husband. Matt took to her immediately.

Overall, it was a wonderful night. Matt handled it all. He did his best and he did great, and I told him so as we drove home. This was his first time mingling in a crowd of strangers, and although I was prepared to go at the slightest hint that he was too overwhelmed, it never got to that point. He did it. He actually did it.

I don't think Fred had the slightest idea of what a big deal this whole night was to my youngest son. He was simply himself: gracious, smiling, laughing, the gentle giant Matt (and I) revered. Thank you, Fred, for pushing me to be my best without ever seeming to push, and thank you also for having that exact same effect on my dear son. You did it all so effortlessly.

As for Matt, well, all I can tell you is that learning never stops, and that is true for everyone whether they are autistic or not. Who knows what the next barrier will be that will come crashing down as Matt continues to grow and navigate his ever-changing environment. One thing I do know? Nothing, it seems, is impossible.

HIS WINGS ARE OPEN,
HE'S READY TO FLY

YESTERDAY WAS ONE of those days that will stay with me forever, locked in my memory, as one of the best days ever. It was almost surreal. It was a day of smiles and conversation and joy, pure joy. I took my twenty-seven-year-old autistic son shopping, which in itself is always fun, but yesterday we were window-shopping for very specific items for his new apartment, and it was especially memorable.

Yes, I really did say that. *Matt's new apartment.* Matt is now on a waiting list for an apartment of his very own. The apartments are exclusively for those who are either disabled or elderly. His label on the spectrum is in the moderate to severe range and he is mostly nonverbal. And he is taking that step toward independence—something every single professional told me would never take place. I stubbornly ignored those negative voices, shut out those disparaging comments about what the future would be like, and listened to only two things: my heart and my son, Matt.

I knew the road would be all uphill. I knew the destination. Goals were set…small, almost insignificant, goals. They were spread out before us, and there were so many that they looked intimidating and, at times, unconquerable. The road forward wasn't even a road back then as we knew absolutely no one who had taken this journey. We were about to embark on an adventure that almost everyone thought we would never finish. Two steps forward, one step back, year after year. Slowly, we made our way up that hill.

The obstacles were many: making eye contact, learning sensory integration, joining in family interactions, allowing social development, teaching me his communication, getting a real education, learning hygiene, cooking, and cleaning, logging his finances, practicing self-sufficiency, and stepping up to take personal responsibility. Oh, the list could go on for miles. We took one day at a time and celebrated even the simplest of accomplishments. We were intensely focused some days and totally oblivious of his autism on other days. There were days he needed to work hard, and there were days where he needed to just flap away and spin. The most important goal was making him feel confident. The more self-esteem he processed, the braver he became. His courage to step into the unknown time and time again never ceased to amaze me.

Then yesterday it hit me, twenty-five years after the onset of autism and his diagnosis, that my youngest son does indeed have a very bright future. We looked at furniture and household goods, and at first he just looked with me. I talked about his new place, his own stuff in his own apartment. I gave him a step by step of what we still needed to do, and I smiled and gave him high-fives. I walked him over to a grouping of simple tables and chairs and stopped. I looked at each one and gave him pros and cons of each then turned and faced my son.

"Which do you like best?" The ball was in his corner. He strode past each, took a deeper interest in how each was made, sat in the chairs, and then turned to me. "I like this one," a huge smile gracing his face. "I love that one!" I replied, running my hand over the glass table and onto the price tag. "Okay, write down the price." Matt took note of the price, and we moved on toward the recliners. For each thing I touched, I would tell him specifics about fabric, taking care of it, the advantages and the disadvantages. Matt would step in and examine each for himself. I continued to lead by example, and Matt continued to thoroughly examine all prospective items and consider his options. Sounds so normal, right?

He spoke yesterday more than he ever has in one day. He talked about the furniture, his plans for his new apartment, and his desires for where he wanted to be ten years from now. He talked about vacations that we would take and places he wanted to see this summer. He talked about shopping for his own groceries. Our next stop was the grocery store close to his soon-to-be new home. He got his own cart and went down specific aisles gathering up the items that make him happy. I shopped separately. We met in one aisle, and he excitedly told me about each item.

Matt has shopped before. He's had a lot of practice under his belt and was eager to show me his skills. He conversed from one store to the next and on the trip home. His words were in stutter form, and some were difficult to release, but he kept at it and never let frustration shut him down. His excitement was so great and his joy so immense that every thought had to released, and I was loving it all. My son said more to me in one day than I had heard in a year.

We talked, we laughed, we walked together in some stores and each on a different path in other stores only to meet up and walk together again. It was the sum of our whole life together in one afternoon. People still ask, "Do you think he is ready?" "Can he really do it?" "Shouldn't he get more practice?" and my all-time favorite, "What will you do after he is gone?"

Ha! First, yes, he is ready. He has been ready, and I have held him back due to finances. We now are financially able to get him started. He has shown immense patience waiting on me. Yes, he can really do this. We have prepared him through years and years of making goals, giving him the tools he needs and showing him we believe in him. He has the confidence to not only try, but also to succeed. No, he has practiced enough, and through his practice, I have seen a young man blossom. There comes a point when practice must be put into action.

And I will be fine. I will be more than fine. I will be the one who sees him through the transition, which will take only a few short years. I will be the one who helps him over the new hurdles, shows him new skills, and cheers him on every single day. I will be the one who pulls back slowly allowing him to not only stretch out those wings, but fly—fly to new heights, to soar confidently on his own. I will be the one who cries the tears of joy as I watched the most amazing person I have ever known beat all the odds. I have fought all his battles with him and have done my best to get him to this point. I am almost finished with being his teacher, and as a teacher, I know when it is time to step away. I will step away slowly, almost imperceptibly, until he is absolutely on his own. Then when he is no longer in need of me as his teacher, I can be who he truly wants me to be, just his best friend.

PARENTAL COURAGE
KNOWING WHEN IT'S TIME
TO ROCK THE BOAT

REVELATIONS COME TO us at various times while parenting. We haven't a how-to manual, and thus as a parent of an autistic young man, I realize that I have made my share of mistakes. I also know that once I acknowledge those mistakes, I can change, whenever I need to. Yes, I can learn from the past and move forward, but sometimes I need a bit of courage. I need that bit of courage to change things up, try something new, be willing to rock the boat if needed. I have a courageous son that shows me how to do it in everything he does. I hope to live up to the high standard of being this young man's mom, and so I gather my courage and prepare to change things. A particular revelation came to me as I contemplated the recent events of the past week. A revelation that now pushes me to rock the boat.

I recently had a friend visit me for a whole week. It was a great experience for me as I hadn't seen my friend in many, many years. We live almost one thousand miles apart, and that means visits are a rarity. Although we talk often on the phone, our last actual face-to-face visit was at least seven to ten years ago. I (and family) saw her last in Illinois. This time she came down to Virginia.

Matt does not remember Carol, my friend of forty-two years. He lost all his childhood memories as he went through puberty and doesn't remember playing at her house, going out to dinner, etc., so I talked to him about her impending visit several times to prepare him for what would be a very big change in his daily routine.

They pulled in last Saturday, and Matt welcomed them (Carol brought her friend Larry) without hesitation, and then proceeded to his game room where he stayed most of the time. Carol is an early-to-bed, early-to-rise kind of person and Matt a late-to-bed, late-to-rise kind of guy. Thus, with opposite schedules, Matt was only subjected to the noise, commotion, and general chaos of the house for about five hours a day. Still, I could tell those five little hours a day were pretty hard on him.

Tough as it may have been, he never once complained. As usual I watched his mannerisms and gestures and body language, and enough silent communication was provided to know the poor guy was feeling stressed. His one moment of excitement was when he was about to go for a drive in Larry's beautiful new copperhead pearl painted 2013 truck. After ten minutes of riding in the backseat next to me, I noticed Matt's face had dropped. He was disappointed by Larry's driving. It wasn't that Larry was a bad driver. He was a cautious driver, braking on every single curve, driving under the speed limit by 10–15 mph, constantly wondering aloud if we were lost (which Matt knew was just not true). But hey, this is Virginia, and those of us who live here have been driving those curvy roads for years. Illinois is flat, roads are generally straight—big, big difference. But I could see Matt was getting quite frustrated. The joyride turned out to be just more stress.

The week flew by, as vacations always do, and he awoke on Friday to find them gone, the house back to normal, and his old routine again made available to him. Matt arose jubilant. His step was light and quick, his smile radiant, and his voice was resonating a happy tone. Life was again good.

There are three things I wish to share with you about this past week's experiences. The first is to again point out just how far he has come—allowing strangers to be around him without meltdown, no show of defiance or anger, no sour disposition. Only one rude comment as Larry was driving when Matt's frustration peaked. He stated, "Larry, you've got to start using your brains!" I took Matt's hand and quietly told him that comment was inappropriate. It wasn't something one said to a guest. Matt has said this to me before, and it's his way of saying "Idiot" but not meant in a mean way.

All in all, I thought he did wonderfully finding his own way to deal with all the new environmental stressors. Understanding his stress level was high, I didn't push him to interact very often.

Then again, I didn't have to. My friend stepped into his life without prompting. She stepped into the world of his game room and initiated conversations. She spoke with him as a young man with wants, thoughts, and feelings. Matt replied, interacted, and was polite. My friend made the first move, knowing that Matt cannot initiate social interaction. She accepted him for who he is and went to him. I was impressed by her ability to get him to respond—just as natural as could be.

And that brings me to the second thing I wanted to share with you. I had an epiphany while watching them interact. I know that no matter how old Matt gets, he will *always* have trouble interacting on a social level. Of course he will. Matt is moderate/severely autistic, and that *fact* will never change. What I find most amazing is my autistic son has more acceptance of other people's lack of communication skills than they have of his.

It all came together as Matt and I were driving to town yesterday and Matt said, "Umm, Larry is a terrible driver. He needed to use his brains. Just terrible, and he can't navigate very well."

Out of the mouth of babes, the truth as Matt saw it. Larry did have trouble driving. He's almost seventy years old, and his vision isn't what it used to be. He was driving on curvy roads where he knew no landmarks, on unfamiliar mountains, and down unfamiliar valleys. I explained all this to Matt. Matt nodded his head solemnly. He understood. Matt's expression of "Poor Larry" said it all. He had accepted Larry's disability (his inability to drive on curvy roads) almost immediately after the explanation. Don't you wish neurotypical people could manage the same thing of autism?

Has it hit you yet? Do you see what is so amazing? Acceptance of a person with autism means accepting who they are—right here, right now. It means understanding there is stress, there is bewilderment, that everything you take for granted in your understanding of life is very frustrating and confusing for them. Acceptance means initiating the conversation. It means not overstepping their boundaries. It means having the *guts* to step out of *your* own comfort zone to initiate a conversation and keep it going. Isn't it strange that Matt can accept fairly easily people who do not act as he thinks they should, and yet it's not like that in reverse? Normal people are not that accepting of those with autism.

Too many people never make that communication attempt. Yes, that includes relatives and a few friends that are so uncomfortable with the thought of autism and so afraid of the communication differences that their only interaction with this wonderful young man is a "Hi, Matt." I stopped trying to force them to accept my son long ago, but I haven't been able to give up on the idea of joint social interaction. As frustrating as it has been, I still try to encourage an interaction, but as the years go by, I am realizing something profound, that it is very difficult for most people to initiate a conversation and keep it going if they don't get the feedback they want. They say their required "hi" and then ignore that he is even around, as if he did not exist, unless he approaches them (which he never will). It makes me want to scream: NEWS FLASH! Matt is autistic!

So I had an epiphany in realizing that the problem with the communication is not so much about my autistic son as it is about those that think they are "normal." Those that seem to have no problem speaking to other people. Until Matt is around. Why is it that these normally vivacious, outgoing, loving people cannot communicate to save their lives when around my autistic son? Why can they not initiate a conversation? Why is Matt just seen but not heard? Is it really that hard?

Which brings me to the third (and last) important item I wanted to share, my own guilt. I have allowed the lack of interaction and the lack of communication—yes, it is my fault. I have always allowed Matt to go off by himself while I interacted with family and friends. I would do the socially acceptable dance of immersing in conversation while my son—my wonderful, accepting son—sat by himself content to play a game or watch TV. I didn't push. I didn't make a scene or stop the presses. I just allowed the time to progress knowing full well that Matt was missing out. Why? Why do people conform to the socially acceptable behavior and sit quietly in the boat when every aspect of their being is screaming to not only rock that boat but tip it plum over? It's about damn time I tipped the boat over.

I am ashamed of myself for the last time. I will no longer sit quietly while my son endures another get-together where he is left out. Maybe I am getting stronger. Maybe I have learned enough to know what is right and what is not. Maybe I have finally found my own courage. Whatever it is, I needed that kick in the pants. I cannot expect others to learn from me if I haven't the *courage* to teach them. I have made up my mind that wherever Matt goes, you will find me also. If he is relegated to watching TV or playing a video at another's house, then I will be there too. I will initiate the conversation just like at home, and I hope I will demonstrate to all those neurotypical people that I love so much but who are afraid of conversing with an autistic young man just how it's done.

I am seeing, really seeing for the first time, that the social interaction and communication deficit is more of a disability for the "normal" person than it is for my son. If Matt can accept a person's differences and still attempt to communicate the best he can (mostly nonverbal) and still wish to be included, then he should be allowed the same respect. Over the years I have found many people will say they "understand" autism but then never so much as attempt to interact or reach out. They are afraid. That is not understanding. It's avoidance.

So I have my work cut out for me as I use my newfound courage to rock the boat. It seems to me that what's missing in our attempts to teach social skills and communication to our autistic children is that we have forgotten that we also need to teach these same skills to those who are neurotypical. If I am going to be successful in gaining autism acceptance for my son, then I will need to first teach those without autism *how* to communicate, and I must do it by example. It's not a matter of them knowing about my son's communication disability. After all, autism is just a word. It's a matter of acceptance of autism, of who he really is. Matt is a real person with all the feelings, thoughts, ideas, and dreams of any other human being. It's something I am afraid others will never realize if they are too uncomfortable to simply sit and talk with him.

Desperate times call for desperate measures. Forget about rocking the boat. It's time to tip the boat over.

JUST ANOTHER DAY
AT THE FLEA MARKET

MATT JUST ATTENDED the Labor Day Flea Market. He *just* walked about, seeking just the right find. Matt was *just* another bargain hunter, one alone in a sea of people that stretched from one end of town to the other. He was *just* one of the five hundred thousand people who attended this year's event. Except, there was no "just" in any of it.

Matt is twenty-seven and moderate to severely autistic and mostly nonverbal. And yet, he walked alone. He bought some items that made him happy. He blended in. No one knew and no one needed to. Matt was able to experience independence like never before. Just another day at the flea market, except it wasn't.

Many people think autism is only a communication and social interaction disorder. For those individuals like my son, autism is so much more than that. Matt was diagnosed with autism so severe the professionals recommended institutionalization. Basically, he was thought to be beyond my reach. Little did his doctors realize just what this mom could do when she is put in such a position (one that many parents like me now know all too well) or about the indomitable spirit of those afflicted with autism.

Over the years, I knew his difficulties in social interaction arose out of his difficulties in communication. Logically one affects the other. When my son, Matt, was just a toddler, he kept to himself and never spoke a word, but over the years, I learned his nonverbal language and he learned mine. In the early years, Matt feared even small gatherings of people. He maintained a personal space that was much larger than most people's, had meltdowns, and cried when it got to be too much—but we never stopped trying. Little by little, year by year, Matt accepted more and more people into his inner circle and even began to enjoy their company. There were always sporting events, picnics, fairs, and flea markets—each of which garnered large gatherings of people, and year by year Matt was exposed to all of them.

One event, the annual Labor Day Flea Market, held in my husband's hometown of Hillsville, brought a massive sea of people together. They came from all over, vendor and bargain hunter alike, and it swelled over the years to encompass the entire town. The flea market has always been a big event for our small family, and in spite of the crowds, we took Matt. We were mindful of his discomfort in those early years and usually carried him through the crowds on our backs or shoulders. Matt eventually grew too heavy for carrying on my back, and at some point, he had to walk alongside me holding my hand. To entice him to go without a fuss, we would bribe him with the promise of buying him a train, and our entire family group kept an eye out for anything railroad related that could bring a smile to my youngest son's face. Anything to make the overwhelming nature of the flea market worth the overstimulation. Year after year we went until one year we noticed Matt was eager to go. From there it just got better.

We've been going to the Labor Day Flea Market now for over twenty years. The week before this year's gathering, I asked Matt if he would like to walk the flea market on his own. He beamed! He could barely believe it. This would be the year that he was finally allowed to walk alone, shop alone, go where he wanted to go, and just blend in. That feeling of freedom must have been immense. I knew in my gut that it was time and he was ready.

I knew because I had prepared him for such things. Matt had experienced shopping in stores alone for years now. He goes one direction as I go another, and when it comes time to go, I call him on his cell phone. He also has experienced purchasing items by himself, be it food or music, toys or clothes. And Matt was excellent about knowing where he was at all times—it is as if he carries a map in his head (I am convinced my son has built-in GPS). So I knew my son was ready because of practice, years and years of practice. The big question really, was I? Was I ready to let go, even for ninety minutes, in a crowd so large?

My son is also a man now. A man that will soon live on his own—something unheard of in the autism community for someone on the moderate to severe end of the spectrum. It's been a long-awaited goal, practiced since way before his high school graduation. His determination drove my determination, and together we knew he was ready to experience independence. His name is currently on the waiting list for an apartment, and we are just waiting for *the call*, the call that will initiate the biggest move of my son's life…and of mine. It's been an exciting and yet scary year (exciting for Matt, scary for me).

So yes, I knew Matt could walk the flea market alone (or I never would have asked him if he wanted to) because I knew in my heart he could. But that does not mean I wasn't scared. Sometimes this mom just needs to let go and have some faith. This was one of those times.

All summer long, Matt reminded me how many days until the flea market on Labor Day weekend. When I announced last week that he could walk it on his own, his joy was overflowing. To prepare him for the big day, I took him shopping to buy him a new watch. Then we made sure his cell phone was charged. Finally, we set a plan in motion of when to meet, how often to call, what to do if someone was mean to him (call me or get a cop). I handed him his allowance for the day, and off we went on a new and exciting adventure.

Our first stop was to see Grandma, who was recovering from surgery in a rehab center one town over from the flea market. Unfortunately, while visiting her, severe storm warning came across the news and the skies turned black. The rain fell in buckets, and the wind bent trees just outside Grandma's window. My heart sank. I looked at Matt. His heart was sinking too.

My stepdaughter, Sarah, and her husband, Paul, had stopped by also. Paul pulled out his smartphone and looked up the weather map. Matt leaned in to examine the situation. When we left, I tried to convince my son it would be okay to go another day, but he wasn't buying it.

As we drove out of town, the rain lessened, and Matt pointed skyward and exclaimed, "It's going away!" "But another storm is coming, Matt. You saw it on Paul's phone, remember?" I replied. "I see a fragment of blue!" he exclaimed and put his thumb and forefinger an inch apart as a measure of the blue and then thrust his measured hope at my face exclaiming, "A fragment!" "But what if it rains while we are there?" I asked tentatively. "Duh… umbrella!" he said, disgusted.

Okay, so I had an umbrella in the back of the jeep. With each mile I drove toward home (and away from the flea market), Matt's frustration escalated. His frustration could not be contained a second longer, and suddenly he smacked his thigh four times with the palm of his hand: *pop, pop, pop, pop.* Those *pops* meant his hopes of going it alone at the flea market were being dashed, and I was the cause.

What was wrong with me? Was I avoiding it for other reasons? Was I…scared? Shouldn't I at least try to be as brave as my son? I pulled into a driveway and turned the jeep around. "I would only do this for you, I'll have you know…" I teased as we headed back toward the town of Hillsville and the hope of the massive flea market. I looked over and smiled. "We will at least give it a try, Matt." With that statement came the resurgence of hope. His face relit with determination, and his eyes became bright once more.

The traffic headed toward town was light, but the traffic headed out was bumper to bumper. Most shoppers were leaving, not wanting to bargain hunt in the rain. We always park in the center of town, and while I easily found a place to park because so many people had left, it had still taken us almost an hour to finally get to that spot. Forty-five minutes waiting in town traffic, and yet his face never showed worry or frustration, only hope. As soon as I cut the engine off, Matt grabbed the umbrella and jumped out. We proceeded down the hill toward the first set of booths. His step was so quick that I found myself trying to keep up with his strides. Excitement permeated the air around him.

"Check your watch. Call me in thirty minutes, okay? Check your cell phone. Let's do a check. Call me," I asked, as if all was great and it was just another, normal day. "Okay," he replied as he took out his phone and pressed the buttons. My phone rang. I opened it. "Hello?" "Hi!" he exclaimed into his phone even though we stood next to each other. "Okay, we're good. Call me at 5:00 p.m. and let me know where you are, please," I said. "Uh, okay," he replied. "Bye, Matt. Have a great time," I said, looking into his bright eyes. "Bye!" Matt replied as he gave me a fist bump then turned and walked away.

And my heart stopped. What if? "Nope—get those what-ifs out of your head, Liz," I reprimanded myself. I turned and forced my legs to walk in the opposite direction. For fifteen minutes I strolled from booth to booth trying to look at various items but not really looking at anything at all. I was too busy forcing myself to just keep going. I rounded a corner, looked up, and there he was, only thirty yards away. He looked right at me, smiled, waved excitedly, then turned and walked away once more. Believe it or not, that was all it took to calm me down—just seeing his face, reading his body language. Matt was just fine. It was exactly what I needed, to see my twenty-seven-year-old autistic son blending in with the massive crowd, confident, happy, and living a dream.

I strolled off again in a different direction, more confident, more at ease.

I began really looking at things and examining items that were appealing, and I started to relax. At five minutes before his first call was due, my phone rang. It was my husband. "How's it going?" he asked immediately. Seems he was just as nervous as I had been ten minutes earlier. We talked a few minutes, but I knew Matt would call exactly at 5:00 p.m., and we kept the conversation short. I hung up and strolled on. At exactly 5:00 p.m., Matt rang my cell phone.

"Hello," I said with a happy voice as if nothing out of the ordinary was occurring. "Hello!" I heard him say in return in an even happier voice. "Where are you?" I asked. "I'm at the Jockey Lot," he replied. Great! He knew his landmarks, and I felt better knowing his internal GPS was working just fine. We made plans to call again in thirty minutes.

Thirty minutes later, I again got my much-needed call, and we planned to meet up at the top of the hill in thirty minutes more. I made record time up the hill to the top and then suffered the wait as I searched the sea of humanity for the light-colored Virginia Tech hat he always wore. When I spotted him, I noted that he was in search mode, looking this way and that, trying to spot my face. I called out and waved. He glanced in my direction, and his face immediately changed from one of worry to one of sheer joy. My heart began to beat once more.

We walked together for a while, ate some ice cream, and slowly strolled back down the hill toward the car, walking side by side. He stopped only once to show me a sign for comic books, and I said I would help him find it the next day. Finally, the Jeep was in sight. We both let out a sigh of relief. I opened the trunk to put in our bags, and as I set my bag down, Matt looked at me and asked, "What did you get?"

I stood stunned for only a moment and then told him of the blue shawl with fringe as I pulled it from the bag to display it.

"That's really cool!" he said as he put his own bags in the trunk next to mine. Matt had *never* asked me what I purchased before. Not ever. His curiosity was as genuine as his approval. As I walked to the driver's side door, I had to fight back a happy dance (with happy tears). Matt had just asked me about something important to me, unexpected and out of the blue. He had just initiated a conversation! This was so much more than a walk around the flea market.

So in all, Matt had spent ninety minutes on his own in the largest gathering to which I could have subjected him. He did so confidently. He knew his way around, purchased some items, and strolled as a free and independent young adult. He blended in and got to feel "normal." My son deserves the right to feel just as free as any other twenty-seven-year-old. His ninety minutes on his own must have felt like heaven. He was so relaxed and so calm upon our return to the car that he even verbally initiated a conversation (first ever). Matt doesn't initiate conversations—at least he didn't until that moment. I will never have to say that phrase again.

The hurdles we face as parents of an autistic child seem never ending, and maybe they are, but as his mom, I say, "So what?" I have learned to jump the hurdles with my son, and now we tackle them almost effortlessly—almost. We may plan for the big hurdles, but we focus on the small ones right in front of us because we know if we can jump those, we can get there—we can jump anything. On Labor Day, two hurdles were cleared: he was able to prove to himself that he could function well in a crowd all on his own, and he initiated a conversation with me without prompting. I would say that all in all it was a very successful day.

We are very hopeful for Matt's future. I have learned to just breathe, just relax, knowing that I can do this, whatever *it* is. It just takes practice. When one thing doesn't work, I just try something new. And slowly over the years, I have learned to just let go, bit by bit. After all, it's just autism, and there's no *just* in any of it.

WALK WITH ME, MATT

"WALK BESIDE ME, Matt." It's a simple phrase and a gentle nudge for my twenty-seven-year-old son to step in line with me as we walk through the store. Matt obliges. His long legs only needed two extra strides, and there he is, on my right-hand side, walking in step with me.

"Remember, Matt, you are an adult, just like me, and you don't need to walk behind me. That's for little kids." As I speak, a mom with three small children go past us, Mom tiredly pushing the shopping cart as her three little ones walk, twirl, and skip behind her. Matt sees the parade before us and looks at me. He smiles. It clicks.

I can't remember when I first walked into a store without carrying my son. I can't remember the first time we walked together with me holding his little hand. These transitions were slow and not really purposeful. They just happened as natural as could be.

I do, however, remember the first time he went into a men's room instead of coming with me to the ladies' room. I remember the fear I had, how my stomach was tied in knots and my mind whirling with all the what-ifs. He was between seven and eight years old. I suppose for a neurotypical child that age, it would not

LIZ BECKER

be extreme to finally allow such a minor event as restroom privacy, but for my son, Matt, who is moderate-to-severely autistic and mostly nonverbal, it was a huge step forward. Allowing him to be on his own, even for a short time, was an extremely stressful event for me.

I remember the first time I let him shop alone. Matt was in his early teens. We were already in the store, and he was right behind me, trailing along as we went from aisle to aisle. I turned around and looked at my son. "Do you want to shop by yourself, Matt?" His face lit up as he examined my face to see if I had really just said that. "Yes!" he replied.

I went over a few ground rules of shopping alone, and off he went, almost skipping with joy. My husband looked at me in disbelief. "I can't believe you just did that," he said worriedly. "Well, he needs to be able to do it, and there's no time like the present to start," I replied, sounding much more sure of my decision than I really was. I remember we made it a game. We shopped for all of five minutes before we went on the hunt for Matt. Once we spotted him, we stayed in the shadows, watching him and giggling like little kids. He was fine. We always found him happily immersed looking over Lego kits, reading magazines, or examining computer games. This was a routine for many months before we stopped hunting and spying and just relaxed and shopped.

I also remember the first time I let him order his own pizza. Matt had just turned twenty. He had always gone in with me to order. Then one day, he used his own ATM card and bought his own pizza. I was there only to help him speak (I told him the words to say). He'd already had many years of practice with his ATM card, and once the words came out, he dipped into his pocket and pulled out his wallet. He fumbled a bit with the wallet, and he stuttered trying to give his order, but he did it. After many months of him giving his own pizza order with a safety net (me), I knew he could do it completely on his own. I never planned it. It just happened. One day when we went for pizza, I unexpectedly changed our routine. I pulled up to the curb and gently nudged him.

"Go ahead, go in and order your pizza by yourself. You know how." Again—his face lit up. He did it…all…by…himself. As he walked back to the car, pizza in hand, he held his head high and strode confidently, as if he had just been given the keys to the kingdom.

Yes, I remember those steps. I remember the way his face lit up every time he took another step toward feeling like a man, the steps that signaled to me that he could be independent if I just walked with him a little while longer, just a little further.

I don't remember the day it dawned on me that my son could do anything—seriously, anything—he put his mind to. Seems I have known it all along, but I still stepped cautiously, waiting for the one hurdle that would stop him. In the back of my mind, I was always prepared for the obstacle that would be too much. The one that would smack me back to the reality of the conventional wisdom of the time, that my severely autistic son would not be able to have a life of independence.

Yet every hurdle to independence was laid down as Matt moved ever forward. Along with every hurdle was another nagging worry. "Would this be the one that keeps him from living on his own?" And time after time, I had worried for nothing. Matt *had* this. What I learned over the years was that the conventional wisdom was completely wrong, and throughout each transition from step A to step B, I stayed hopeful. I never thought about what my son couldn't do, only about what he could.

As we traveled up one hill and down another to get to where we are today (Matt will soon be moving to his own apartment), I found that one of hardest obstacles on our road was simply being able to convey the meaning of the sentiment "different, not less." Matt, with all his great strides toward getting to this point, had never really viewed himself as equal. For years and years I searched for a way to make him understand that his autism didn't

make him *less* of a person. Although I had given him encouragement at every turn and taught him the skills he needed to fly on
his own, I hadn't gotten it through to him that he was not less for
having autism. Matt hates it so. But the truth is being autistic did
make him feel less, so he tried hard to do the socially acceptable
behaviors, make the socially acceptable replies, and he watched
others, the neurotypical people, as his role models on how to get
him there, to the place where he could feel not less, but equal. It's
okay for my son to be autistic. It's okay for him to not want to be.
But it's not okay for him to feel less because of it. So maybe you
can imagine how bad I felt when it dawned on me that when my
son walked behind me, even by just one step, he was signaling to
me that he felt less.

I don't remember when I embarked on trying to break that
nasty habit, only that it has taken years. I would wait for him to
step next me, but as soon as I would begin to walk again, Matt

would routinely wait a fraction of second so he could follow. Again I would stop and wait. We would take a few steps together, and then his gait would slow—just a second—and I would be leading once again. It must have appeared to others witnessing our interaction as some sort of strange dance. Stop and wait, stop and wait, stop and wait. The goal was for him to walk beside me without my asking. Matt read my body language as he always did, but this change confused him. The years came and went, and even though it still remained a long-sought-after prize, the dance did seem to get a bit smoother. I considered my "gently nudging my son to walk *with* me" as a type of dance practice. Someday, I hoped, someday my son would feel the need to walk beside me, and this silly dance would be over.

Even though I don't remember the first time I asked him to walk beside me, I do remember how he felt each time he did. I remember how simply being asked was viewed as such an honor, and how his face lit up just like it did when he was given the chance to go on his own to the restroom, to shop alone, and to order his own pizza. Always happy to oblige, he would take a few large steps and slide in beside me with a smile on his face. But it never lasted very long, and after a few brief moments in the sun, he would revert to his old routine and follow me instead, and his smile would dim.

It's was the need for an invitation that was a thorn under my skin. I could *see* that when he walked behind me that he didn't carry himself with that same sense of purpose, and he didn't shine with that wonderful confidence that he exudes when we would walk together—for when he walked beside me, he glowed. It emerged without constraint, emanating from his being unfettered, and as natural as breathing. We were just two adults walking together, side by side, equals. For a young man who has used nonverbal communication to "speak" to me his whole life, this simple form of body language conveyed immense amounts of feeling and emotion to me.

So I just kept nudging, "Walk with me?" regardless of whether we hiked a trail, shopped in a mall, or simply went for a walk down our road. I yearned for my dear son to please just walk *with* me. I wanted him to feel it naturally, to fall in step without my asking, and at the onset of each opportunity, I begged silently, "Come on, Matt, just step right up next to me and match me stride for stride. I know you can do this," and I then waited to see if maybe this time he would.

It's such a little thing, I suppose, but it was important to me. It was important to Matt too; he just didn't realize it yet. As time went on, it became my obsession. I didn't just want him to walk with me anymore. I *needed* him to. When you live with someone who is mostly nonverbal, you read every other form of communication, not the least of which was body language. I just knew if he could do it naturally, without prodding, that his body language would reveal that powerful message, a feeling of equality. I just knew that in the initiation of that one simple movement of stepping in beside me without being asked (and staying there), he would be telling me he felt *whole*. I believed that in that one movement, he would reveal an unconscious affirmation of his own self-worth.

So when Matt saw that mother of three parade past us in the store, I knew he understood. It was in his eyes. It was in his smile. It clicked. Matt realized he was no longer that little kid his mom fretted over if he was more than two feet away. He was no longer that child his mom spied on as he shopped on his own. He wasn't the kid whose mom ordered pizza for him. He was an adult, a soon to be an on-his-own adult, and he became empowered. Matt took another large step, and we continued on through the store, side by side. I never nudged him again.

My son realized, thankfully, that he was equal. He was in charge of where he wanted to go. His destiny was in his hands. Sure, he was autistic, but he was okay. Different, but not less, never less. Body language is powerful stuff. Nowhere is the sense of equality portrayed any clearer than in how one walks with another. That simple phrase first spoken by Temple Grandin is not just about whether someone neurotypical thinks of someone autistic as *different, not less*. It's also about how the autistic individual feels about themselves.

It's been a hurdle, one much harder to clear than it sounds. Matt now walks *with* me, matching me stride for stride, confident, head held high, and a smile on his face everywhere we go. And he does so without my nudging him, without hesitation, and he stays in step. You can be sure there's a smile on my face too as I feel the power of that movement, the underlying confidence radiates from my son's very soul. Yes, he's different, but not less.

He gets it. He is…equal.

A HOME OF HIS OWN

IT WAS A wonderful evening. My son, Matt, was cooking ham-
burgers on his new electric grill in the kitchen while his siblings
and their spouses were in the living room laughing and conversing with my husband, Tom. I was with Matt, helping him to play
the role of host. You see, this was no ordinary party. This was a
house-warming party for Matt. We had just completed putting
his new apartment together that very afternoon. It was a party
twenty-five years in the making, and each one of us was now a
witness to the impossible. Matt's dream of living on his own was
finally coming true.

Matt is almost twenty-eight years old. He was diagnosed
at the age of two as moderate/severe autistic, and that hasn't
changed. Although he speaks on occasion, he is mostly nonverbal
and relies on other forms of communication: facial expression,
gesture, and body language. He is highly sensitive to loud sounds,
bright lights, strong smells, and various textures and temperatures.
His heightened senses were so very hard for him as a young child,
but he found a way to deal with his sensitivities and now handles
the onslaught of environmental stimuli very well. The severity of
his autism meant the chances of him one day living on his own,

in a place of his very own, was basically zero. This is a young man who twenty-five years ago should have been institutionalized, at least the specialists all thought so. That was back in 1988, when autism was rare (1:10,000), and they assumed it would be more than I could bear, more than my family could handle, too much of a strain for all involved, but they were all wrong. Needless to say, Matt came home with me from his weeklong evaluation, rejoined his family, and our journey with autism began in earnest.

Is it no wonder then that I was amazed by my son every single day? Is it no wonder that each tiny, minute step forward was a cause for celebration? The first time his eyes met mine, the first time he called me "Mama," the first time he wrote his name, read a book, played with his brother Christopher. The first time he threw a ball, participated on a team (T-ball), sat at a desk, touched my face to comfort me, bought a gift for another person, said "I love you," made the honor roll at school, ordered his own pizza, cooked his own meal, or washed his own clothes. The list is as long as his life. Each step was a powerful reminder of his courage and determination, and the hope for his future stayed with me.

With a diagnosis of autism and grim predictions from the specialists, was it any wonder that I worried over his future? What would happen to this precious little boy if something happened to me? Would they put him away like an unwanted toy and forget him? Even though the years sped by, that fear remained. What I needed was simply time. I knew I could get him to independence, to that one magnificent goal, if I just had enough time. The road has been a long one, of course it has, because nothing goes fast when you're dealing with autism.

Over the years I set goals and watched in amazement as he met them, day by day, month by month, and year by year. How quickly he met the goal was not the issue, but whether he could do it at all. Some goals took decades, like speech. Others lasted only a few days, like alternating his feet when he climbed stairs.

For most goals, the progress was slow and steady, at a snail's pace. But after witnessing a few thousand miracles, you realize the time it took to get to the miracle just didn't matter. And so we pressed onward, day by day, month by month, and year by year.

But even a slow pace wouldn't have worked if I had not been open to learning about my son—his cues, his preferred forms of communication—and accept him for who he was. He was not like anyone I had ever known, and in the beginning I had to resist the temptation to force him to fit into a mold made for the neurotypical. Thankfully, I realized early on there was no reason to force him into any mold, for any label, for no mold could've contained him. Matt was unique to the world, and I needed to allow myself to follow just as much as I led. I learned early on what my role in his success would be. I understood, almost instinctively, that I was not just his teacher showing him how to button a shirt, hold a pencil, or in later years, use a stove. I was also his student, learning through observation, deciphering hidden meanings, and empathizing with him at every turn. If he were hiding behind a chair, then I sat there too, with him, taking in the surroundings, the feel of the place, the lighting, and the sounds. If he repeatedly drew the same design on paper, then I hunted for what it meant until I figured it out. Matt was my biggest mystery, and I was his biggest fan. Together we navigated the rough seas of autism, but we also drifted beside beautiful shores where we could see a future filled with smiles and joy and independence. All the signs were there. We just needed time.

My wonderful, amazing son has wanted a home of his own since he was nineteen years old. For ten long years, he has worked ever so hard to get the skills to live on his own. And then one day last April, I realized Matt was ready to attempt it. The knowledge just came to the surface of my mind, and I couldn't shake it. I have known for several years that he was ready to try his wings. For the past several years, I had tested him repeatedly, found a few areas of concern, and made those concerns evaporate through setting and reaching new goals. Now the only goals that remained were those involved in the day-to-day challenges of actually living on his own, and I couldn't deal with those until he was actually on his own. The time for the transition to independence had arrived.

Finding the right place was our next step. It had to be perfect—and I do mean perfect. It had to be safe, and it had to be conducive to Matt's special needs. I found such a place, an apartment complex specifically for the elderly and disabled. Nice little duplexes snuggled in a cul-de-sac, bordered by pine trees and maintained with high standards. It was income subsidized and private. Matt was put on the waiting list with a four-to-six-month wait. That gave us more time, time to get his furniture together and gather household items, time to save money for his bills, time to simply adjust to the idea that a big change was coming.

As it turned out, I had eight months to prepare myself, and I honestly thought I was—until the call came. I was talking on the phone with Tom when my call waiting beeped. I thought it was the mechanic with news about my Jeep and asked Tom to hold a second while I took the call. As soon as I heard her voice, I knew who it was and I knew why she was calling. Before her words could land on my ears, my legs began to shake and tears began clouding my vision.

"Hi, Liz, this is Rhonda. We have an apartment available for Matt," she stated happily. I somehow managed to make the appointment to sign the lease, thanked her, and said good-bye, then clicked back over to Tom.

"Tom? Matt just got his apartment." Then I started to *really* cry. Tom was caught off guard. He was silent for only a moment (from shock) and then also began to cry. It was finally here. The day was set. The transition to independence would begin in ten days. All of a sudden, I didn't feel so ready anymore. What if I was doing this too soon? What if he needed more practice? What if he couldn't do it? For the first time since Matt's diagnosis, I really doubted myself. How will I be able to do this? What if somebody hurt him? What if… Oh, the enormity of the what-ifs.

I dried my face, took a breath in and out, and told Matt about his apartment. Matt, eager to move, ready to move, and thrilled to move, danced around and thrust both fists toward the sky. "Yes!" he exclaimed over and over. I smiled. Matt's moment of joy completely took center stage. I knew deep down that of course he could do this, but it still took a few days for me to feel that same joy and confidence. I had to wade through my grief and my fear first—grief in having this wonderful young man move away from me and fear of the what if.

I summoned all my courage and got busy helping him to label his boxes, make a move-in schedule, and put a plan in place for how exactly to do it all that would give Matt a sense of empowerment, and yet, not overwhelm him with the change. Thankfully, the apartment was ready before the date given and we were given access to it a week early, a blessing in disguise. I took that chance to slowly move boxes over, slowly get him used to going over there and using his new key. He was so excited about opening that door the first time that he fumbled the key a bit but then stepped eagerly into his new apartment. When we left that day, we went immediately to get new keys made—one each for me, Tom, and his big brother, Christopher. As we walked out of the store, I realized Matt was no longer smiling. It took a bit of questioning before he revealed to me he was scared. It had finally hit him…he was moving away.

Moving away for the first time, to a new place, a new area of town with new surroundings and feeling unsure of oneself is a pretty natural response, I think. All he needed was support, a schedule, and time, lots and lots of time. Once Matt realized that he didn't have to leave that very day, his smile returned and he calmed down. He started marking the days on a calendar, the countdown to his first overnight in his new place.

After a day at home on a normal schedule, Tom and Matt started carrying boxes over to his new apartment while I was at work. Tom told me later that Matt looked totally dazed, not knowing what to do with room after room of boxes. He told Matt not to worry, that Mama had this. He said Matt smiled immediately and calmed right down. He asked for another day off, just a nice, normal routine day, before packing and moving boxes again. He needed time to take it all in. The change was hard, and his day-to-day routines were being threatened. We took a few days off.

Tom had to work the day we move the furniture and my Jeep was in the shop. I was more than stressed. That's when my step-daughter, Sarah, her husband Paul, and Christopher came to the rescue, bringing two trailers and a truck. As I waited for their arrival that morning, I had an epiphany. I had been thinking about how huge this was and how this day would be the biggest day of his life, Matt's biggest challenge. I said it out loud as I looked at my reflection in the bathroom mirror. Then the thought occurred to me, that heck, it was the biggest challenge of my life too, but realized in a fraction of a second that that just wasn't true. I corrected myself immediately.

You see, twenty-nine years ago this same week, I held my newborn son Daniel in my arms and watched the heart moni-tor mark his last heartbeat. *That* was the hardest day of my life. My biggest challenge was to go on living without him. I realized that Matt's move, while extremely stressful for Matt, was not all that hard for me. I had survived the death of a child, and when I eventually, finally reentered the world, I knew I was stronger. Matt was born the next year, and I knew I could handle anything life handed out, *anything*, except the death of another child.

That was why his autism never fazed me—after all, there are worse things. That's also why I was never in a hurry to complete a goal, never needed to make him fit a mold. I knew, in that instant, staring in the mirror, that I could do this, and if I remained strong, then Matt could do this. He got his strength from me, and if I waivered even a little, his courage would fade. I reminded myself that this move was not about sadness in him leaving. It was about celebrating that he could leave. I knew in an instant that not only could I do this, I could also do this with my hands tied behind my back and blindfolded. My son needed me, and I would walk through fire if that's what it took to keep him focused and calm. I looked back at my reflection in the bathroom mirror, "You got this, Liz," and I did. My grief at the idea of him leaving dissipated into thin air, and I was once again myself.

The kids arrived shortly after, and we started hauling furniture that I had saved and collected over the years, more boxes, and even the cabinets that I remade into end tables. His siblings were fast and efficient and in high spirits. Before we knew it, they were gone, and Matt and I were alone staring at an apartment of boxes and furniture and general chaos. The rest of the day it was just him and me and an apartment in dire need of organization.

"Matt, first, we divide the boxes into their rooms," and immediately he began picking up boxes, reading the labels and taking them to the correct rooms. Then we moved furniture to the locations of his choice. "Where do you want this, Matt, here or here?" Giving him choices narrowed his focus, and before you knew it, all the furniture was in place, tables placed, book cases assembled, books on shelves, and a kitchen with actual cookware, plates, cups, and silverware all neatly stored. Matt was a part of every decision, allowing him total control on how his new place would look and feel. After hours of organizing and assembling, we needed a break, so we went grocery shopping to fill his fridge, which was pretty easy as he still only eats fifteen foods. We also bought some cleaning supplies, and when we had all the food stored, we cleaned surfaces, drawers, shelves, TV, etc. Then back to putting a bathroom together and finally the bed. Matt assembled the bed by himself, just as he had the bookcase—all those Lego schematics he had read over the years had really paid off.

He read the schematic and piece by piece put his bed together without any help from me. As I viewed the finished product, I puffed up with enormous pride. I helped him to make his bed and then moved on to hanging his curtains. In hanging curtains, I asked Matt to tell me when the rod was level—something he can eyeball perfectly.

When we left for the day, his apartment had really changed from one of complete chaos to a very nice Matt man-cave, completely decorated in his favorite Virginia Tech colors of orange and maroon. As we drove out of town, Matt told me he needed a few more days off. We made plans for two days later, on Tuesday (his official house-warming day), to finish up. Matt needed time to reboot. It was all so much, and even with going over only every other day, the pace was too fast. We needed to slow down, to a snail's pace if possible, because after all, it was a huge deviation from his normal routine. Matt chose the schedule he needed, and I understood. We were not in any hurry.

When Tuesday morning arrived, Matt and I put the last of his beloved books in the car and went back inside to wait for Tom to get home. Matt walked slowly to his old game room and stood in the doorway and looked around. It was now just an empty room with dust bunnies and a few odds and ends of things that would remain. I put my arms around his shoulders. "It's all going to be okay, Matt." He turned and hugged me. He was doing all he could to just keep focused on the task at hand, but he was nervous. His old routines were being altered one by one, and the stress was almost overwhelming. His most important routine occurs each night as the sun goes down. Matt needs his books around him at night—about thirty manga books piled neatly on three sides of the bed, surrounding him and shielding him from the fear of the dark. He could not sleep in his new place without that nightly ritual, so the last thing he took was his books. He was ready.

We met Christopher and his sweetheart, Jessie, in town and headed over to Matt's place. His brother programmed the TV and helped Matt hang his posters. We finished with small odds and ends as his other siblings arrived and marveled at the beautiful way Matt had decorated. Matt opened more presents, cooked us dinner, and tried very hard to be a good host. 'Round about 9:00 p.m., he was winding down. His eyes had that half-open look, and he was spending more time in his bedroom away from everyone. That was Tom's cue to get going, and all the kids took the hint and said their good-byes. With everyone gone but Matt and I, we kicked back, put on a movie, and just relaxed. After the movie, he went back to his bedroom again to lay out all his books. I went and put on my pajamas, and as I came out of the bathroom, I saw him sitting on the edge of his bed flipping channels with the TV remote. I couldn't help it. I ran and jumped on his bed, landing behind him, and put my arms around him and hugged him. Matt instinctively relaxed backward into the embrace, put his arms over mine, and we sat there like that and watched the last moments of *Ghostbusters* together. His leaning into me touched my heart. I could feel the love, the "Thanks, Mom" that I knew he couldn't say. The feel of him in my arms was all I needed to know he was happy, proud of himself, and thankful not to be alone that first night. It was so very hard to let go.

The stress of change has been too much, and although we go over every day, he can't bring himself to stay there overnight more than once a week, but I expected that. It's just not that big of a deal how often he spends the night alone. It's a transition, and this particular transition will be a slow one. I'm still in awe that the transition has begun. Of course it's going to be a long road, and sure, the pace will be slow, but the goal that has been set is a wonderful, almost inconceivable goal. It's not like dropping your kids off at college. It's not like the "moving away" that most people envision. It's a transition, and as with all things autism, this transition will take time, lots of time.

It doesn't matter how fast he is acclimated to his new surroundings. It's that he is attempting it at all that counts. That's the miracle. That's what touches my soul. So it just doesn't matter if he only stays one night a week, because in time he will move it to two, then to three, and one day, maybe six months from now, or maybe next year, Matt will live on his own completely…in a home of his very own.

Amazing.

EPILOGUE

Matt continues to progress in his quest to be and feel totally independent. Each week since November of 2013, we have discovered something new to work on; social interaction with neighbors, walking to his local grocery store alone, planning his days and even bravely combatting one of his biggest fears—darkness—when the power went out for an hour one night.

His move to his new place is not the end of the story but the beginning of a new chapter on how to transition to independence. As we all know, everything in autism requires time and patience—transitioning is no different.

Matt started out spending just one night a week at his new place, but that arrangement didn't last long. Within a few months, Matt had already adjusted to his new surroundings and increased his time at his place in small increments up to the six days a week he spends there now. It's obvious to me how much he loves his own place, how confident he feels, and how determined he is to be successful.

It's a good thing I'm keeping notes as to all the seemingly minor needs of my autistic son living independently as one day soon, I will be able to share these new insights with my readers in another book—on transitioning.

And so, the story continues…